Think & Grow
Christ-Minded

&

Sonship Lifestyle:
A Mission-Minded Lifestyle Manual

MISSIONARY PAULYB

ACKNOWLEDGMENTS

This book was a labor of love. Love for the GODHEAD and my fellow man.

Thank you for all who supported me in creating this book.

To my wife, Stellah, you are the love of my life. Thank you for always standing by me.

To my amazing beautiful children, Naomi, Job and Lovie, you are my blessings.

To my friend, Pete Cabrera, Jr.

To Robert & Jessica Eddowes of Revel8ion Media for editing.

To Antonio Torres, thank you for the encouragement as a friend.

To Sheila Parnell for editing, designing the cover and for helping make this book amazing.

To Kelley Chance and Phil Parnell for their assistance in editing.

To Catherine Mbula Kitaka of Nairobi, Kenya for her assistance in editing.

CONTENTS

SECTION ONE

Think & Grow Christ-Minded

CHAPTER ONE

ONENESS

What Does This Mean?

As sons of God, we have been born into a unique partnership with the divine Godhead. The nature of the Father, the Son and the Holy Spirit allows us to grow in Christ through His sacrifice. He is in us.

Part of growing in Christ is in taking on the mindset of Jesus. We do this by learning and understanding our divine nature in our oneness with the Father. We also take on the mindset of Jesus by cultivating a relationship with the Holy Spirit and allowing Him to permeate all aspects of our being.

We can understand the very mind of Jesus, which is rooted in the divine nature of God, by capturing the mind of the Spirit. This brings us into a greater understanding of who He is in us, and the divine nature we carry in Christ Jesus. Every believer can grow and flow from this mindset that is rooted in the Spirit of the Father's divinity.

> *"Let this mind be in you, which was also in Christ Jesus: Who, being in the form of God, thought it not robbery to be equal with God." Philippians 2:5 (KJV).*

The above scripture tells us that we have been brought into oneness with the divine nature of the Trinity.

We have been made one with Abba Father; as equal right shareholders in Christ Jesus. Being sons of the Father, we are to live like Christ in unity and in likeness of the divine nature of the supreme Father, Who is Spirit.

Let us begin by laying down some groundwork. The following scripture will help us in this journey of discovering what it means to be in oneness with God.

> *"Most assuredly, I say to you, he who hears My word and believes in Him who sent Me has everlasting life, and shall not come into judgment, but has passed from death into life." John 5:24.*

> *"One God and Father of all, who is over all and through all and in all." Ephesians 4:6 (NASB).*

> *"But he who is joined to the Lord is one spirit with Him." 1 Corinthians 6:17.*

Food for thought: I always ask our students, what would your life look like if you really believed in the knowledge you know?

These verses should bring us comfort when we read about how we have passed from death to life. (Read Romans 6:1-6).

At our born-again experience, the Spirit of God literally transferred us from death into life. This means life is in you, in me and in us!

To further understand this let's look at what type of bodies there are.

> *"There are also celestial bodies and bodies terrestrial; but the glory of the celestial is one, and the glory of the terrestrial is another." 1 Corinthians 15:40 (KJV).*

The line "there are celestial bodies and terrestrial bodies" is very important for us to understand. The verse shows that there are two different kinds of bodies; celestial and terrestrial. It is important that we understand that there is a natural body and a supernatural spirit body.

> *"It is sown a natural body; it is raised a spiritual body. There is a natural body, and there is a spiritual body." 1 Corinthians 15:44 (KJV).*

Verse 45 says: *"So, it is written, 'the first man Adam became a living being.' The last Adam (referring to Jesus) became a life-giving spirit."* (1

Corinthians 15:45, KJV). Furthermore, *"He who believes My words and in Him who sent Me has eternal life."* (John 5:24). *"So, as God has life in himself, so the Son has life in Himself."* (John 5:26).

Read carefully Romans 8: 9-11.

Since the Father has life, Jesus too has life as His Son. The moment we believed in Jesus, we became sons of God and became one in the Spirit. This same Spirit quickens us to understand the things of God and everything we have inherited. He quickens us to not only understand everything Jesus is, but also ultimately everything that we have inherited through Christ as sons of God.

This truth must become our reality, as we are life-giving celestial sons of God, just like Jesus.

> *"But you are not in the flesh but in the Spirit, if indeed the spirit of God dwells in you. Now if anyone does not have the Spirit of Christ he is not His."* Romans 8:9.

The Bible emphasizes this oneness by stating: *But the person who is joined to the Lord is one spirit with Him.* I Corinthians 6:17.

Wherever we go, we give life to those who are dead. We breathe this spirit into them and they receive what we have received thereby igniting the fire of the Spirit in their lives. The Spirit of Jesus says He is the giver of life.

> *"As the living Father sent Me, and I live because of the Father, so he who eats Me, he also will live because of Me. This is the bread which came down out of heaven; not as your fathers ate and died; he who eats this bread will live forever."* John 6:57-58.

When we are in Christ, we have passed from death and condemnation into life everlasting. Death is rooted in the fallen nature of the "old man" or the flesh. The fallen nature and death no longer dominates us or has lordship over us, because the old man's nature is dead and the Spirit's life in us has taken over uniting us in spirit, soul and body.

3

"The first man [Adam] is of the earth, earthly [terrestrial]: and the second Man [Jesus] is the Lord from heaven [celestial]. As is the earthly; such are they also that are earthly: and as is the heavenly, such are they also that are heavenly." And as we have borne the image of the earthly, we shall also bear the image of the heavenly." I Corinthians 15:47-48.

Paul, the Apostle, is talking about us, who are born of the Spirit. God's Children are spirit just like God is Spirit. Those who are born-again are of heaven and have life. Those who are not born-again are of the earth, carnality, fleshly and sensual. God didn't come to divide the natural part of you from the spirit. He came to unite you into one complete person in the Spirit of God's reality of truth in the world.

Mindset of Heaven

Those who are of this world have the law of death functioning in them because every man who is born into this world is born after the first Adam.

"The law of the spirit of life in Christ Jesus has set you free from the law of sin and death." Romans 8:2.

So, is it safe to say that "life" is a person, and the image of the person is the spirit? There is a law of life that is in Christ Jesus for everyone who believes.

"For to be carnally minded is death; but to be spiritually minded is life and peace." Romans 8:6.

Jesus spoke of life after death when he went to raise Lazarus: *"Jesus told her, 'I am the resurrection and the life. Anyone who believes in Me will live, even after dying. Everyone who lives in Me and believes in Me will never ever die. Do you believe this, Martha?'"* (John 11:25).

In the Gospel of John, Jesus explained His salvation mission and what happens when we are born again.

4

"I tell you the solemn truth, the one who hears My message and believes the one who sent Me has eternal life and will not be condemned but has crossed over from death to life. I tell you the solemn truth, a time is coming-and is now here-when the dead will hear the voice of the Son of God, and those who hear will live." John 5:24-25.

The only one who gives life, even after death, is Christ. By believing that He is the savior of the world, we have eternal life. He conquered and defeated death to give us life in abundance. This is why Jesus said you must be born-again out of the second and last Adam. Otherwise, those who have not been born of the second and last man, Jesus Christ, are born with the law of death working in them.

When we believe the law of Christ, instantly we can know that heaven and life are now at work in us. With that commitment, we receive the second and last Adam, Jesus Christ, who is full of life.

In Romans, the Bible says that the law of the first man, Adam, who is rooted in sin and death, has been set free by the second and last Adam, into the law of life in the Spirit and in liberty. So, we now live by the faith of the Son of God in our body/flesh. (Galatians 2:20).

"The law of the Spirit of life in Christ Jesus has set you free from the law of sin and of death." Romans 8:2.

The Bible explains that Jesus rose from the dead so that we may acquire the new life.

"Therefore, we have been buried with Him through baptism into death, so that as Christ was raised from the dead through the glory of the Father, so we too might walk in newness of life." Romans 6:14.

The scripture further shows the source of the liberty (freedom) we walk in after being born in the new life.

"Now the Lord is the Spirit, and where the Spirit of the Lord is, there is freedom." 2 Corinthians 3:17.

There is a primary purpose for sharing this so we can understand there is a mindset that is necessary for everyone who is born of God.

This mind is in the Spirit. For us to know the Father we must know Him in His likeness and image which is through the Spirit. We need to *let this mind be in you that was also in Christ Jesus.* (Philippians 2:5-9).

Jesus Christ, even after being born as a man, living in the same world that we are living in, never conformed His mindset to what was surrounding Him because the mindset He had was "who His Father was" and "who He [God] said" Jesus was.

So, if we have the mind of Christ Jesus then we will know our identity is based on the identity of the Godhead and what they are saying, not what our ego, religion or the opinions of others tell us.

> *...and a voice from heaven said, 'This is my Son, whom I love; with Him I am well pleased.' Matthew 3:17.*

That is the mindset that was in Jesus. He knew His image, identity, and mindset was of the Spirit and who He was as a Son in the Father. Despite all this, He still humbled Himself.

But we cannot separate who Jesus is in the Father. Jesus Christ in all His humility understood His equality in oneness with the Spirit, nature and the mindset of the Father as the Son of God. In layman terms, what Jesus was saying is that "in My mindset, I am one with the Father - We function in unity." He could say this even while He was 100% God and 100% man. (Phil 2:5-8). Also, when we are born into Christ Jesus we too are 100% of that Divine union and 100% man just like Jesus in oneness.

I suggest you read John Chapter 17 because it reveals the heart of Jesus and the Father. It also gives you a portrait of what oneness looks like. (1 John 4:17).

In the following diagram you can write your name at the center of it to illustrate your placement in the very nature of the Father, Son, and Holy Spirit.

Our Oneness In the Nature Of the Godhead

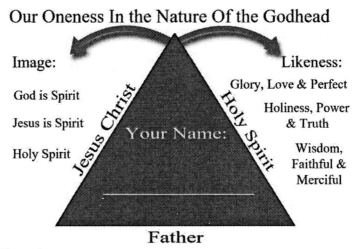

Image:

God is Spirit

Jesus is Spirit

Holy Spirit

Jesus Christ

Your Name:

Holy Spirit

Likeness:

Glory, Love & Perfect

Holiness, Power & Truth

Wisdom, Faithful & Merciful

Father

Figure 1

"For by these He has granted to us His precious and magnificent promises, so that by them you may become partakers of the divine nature, having escaped the corruption that is in the world by lust." 2 Peter 1:4.

To fully paint a picture of the likeness and the image of God in us, a few characteristics of God's nature are listed above in Figure 1. Some are holiness, power, truth etc.

The key point here is to understand that the image and likeness described in the diagram is within us. There is nothing missing or lacking. By understanding this, we can start living from a place of peace and security.

What would our life look like if we really believed in what we know to be truth?

Let us think of ourselves as sons of God who has the very nature of God's likeness. Understanding this truth is more than knowledge, it is to begin walking in it by renewing our minds. God is Spirit which is eternal. Sons of God are capable of functioning from this eternal nature of God. They are created in their Dad's image and likeness which is in spirit.

Do not lie to one another, seeing that you have put off the old self with its practices and have put on the new self, which is being renewed in knowledge after the image of its creator. Colossians 3:9-10.

Jesus told the religious leaders He could only do what He saw the Father doing. (John 5:19). What Jesus was really saying is that He "thinks like His Father thinks." In another verse, he says: *"I and the Father are one."* John 10:30.

What Jesus is not saying is that He is the Father. However, He is saying that He is one with the Father as the Son of God.

There are three persons having the same likeness and mindset: God the Father, Jesus Christ the Son, and Holy Spirit.

Everything Jesus or the Holy Spirit does, they do it in agreement with God's nature. They will not do anything contrary to the Father's will. Therefore, what we do should also be in the same mindset with the nature of the Father.

Jesus told the Father, I have given to them the glory and honor which You have given Me, that they may be one as We are One: I in them and You in Me, in order that they may become one and perfectly united, that the world may know that you sent Me. (John 17:22). The Father gave Jesus what He had asked for…to share His glory in oneness.

Religion has taught us that if we think we can share God's glory that we are being prideful and are stealing His glory. But ponder this question: How can you steal God's glory if He gave it to you?

It is important to take note that Jesus made it clear that we share in the oneness that is between the Father and the Son. As one with Jesus we are rooted in the image and likeness of the nature of Father God which includes His glory. The Holy Spirit has transformed us to this likeness.

This is the mindset that the sons of God are to have - knowing it is a privilege to live in Christ Jesus. This mindset is our inherited, heavenly, divine origin as sons.

The Apostle Paul speaks of where Christ places us as sons of God:

> *And raised us up with Him and seated us with Him in the heavenly places in Christ Jesus, so that in the ages to come He might show the surpassing riches of His grace in kindness toward us in Christ Jesus." Ephesians 2:6-7.*

> *If ye then be risen with Christ, seek those things which are above, where Christ sitteth on the right hand of God. Colossians 3:1 (KJV).*

We are to have the mindset of heaven which is rooted in the Spirit of God.

Why Seek Things Above?

We should seek the things above because we are seated in Christ Jesus at the right hand of the Father. But, sometimes it's difficult to fully comprehend our identity in Christ and what it looks like, without first capturing who Jesus is and who we are in Him. So, in the next few chapters, I'm going to help you get some basic understanding that will catapult your future in the kingdom of God.

Paul said: *"It's no longer I who live but is Christ who lives in me."* (Galatians 2:20). Meaning, it's not about us in the flesh; rather it is about us in Christ as spiritual sons and learning to function from the place of the Spirit.

God unites us spirit, soul and body and even our feelings and emotions are in Him. He is our coach, teaching us how to align our natural realities to His kingdom realities. We are not flesh, we are spirit. (Roman 8:9).

CHAPTER TWO

DISCOVERING YOUR ROOTS

Core Identity

Let's start discovering our root. When God created Adam and Eve He made them with His image in mind.

So, the question here is what is the image of God? Many will say Jesus. Yes, that is true but what is the image of Christ? Many will say the Father. But, my question would be better stated, what is the image and the likeness of Jesus and the Father? What unifies them as one?

Our answer is found in John 4:24 where it says that God is Spirit. Also, in Romans 8:9 it gives this perspective, "*you are not in the flesh* (old man nature)". There is a reality check here. This is actually saying that when we live in the flesh it is a false identity rooted in the fallen nature of the first Adam; this isn't who you are as sons of God. It does however say "you are spirit". The core foundation of your identity is the Spirit of God; it's your identification card that classifies you as a son or daughter of God. Paul says in Romans 8:11b that the Spirit gives life to your mortal body which means all of you, including your body/flesh.

You (self, ego, mind, spirit) are one with Them in Spirit. (1 Corinthians 6:17). This verse says you are identified as a son/daughter of God because you're born of and united with Them in Spirit.

Here is some food for thought concerning God's design for unity. Before the fall, Adam and Eve were called man and woman. They both only had one name, Adam. (Genesis 5:2). They were one. Actually, Eve wasn't even given the name Eve until after the fall. That's when Adam identified her as separate from himself. (Genesis 3:20). Their identity changed between each other when their identity changed with God…no longer one.

11

Note: Before our born-again experience, the old man (flesh) nature is what divided man's spirit, soul and body. But, Jesus brought life and united the complete man into Himself. If the mindset of the old man doesn't understand that he's dead then he is positioned to be tricked into believing another gospel. (2 Corinthians 11:3-5).

Adam and Eve viewed everything according to God in the reality of His Spirit. In fact, everything in the lives of Adam and Eve were perfect. I say this because to be in the garden with God and to have fellowship with Him would have to be from the perspective of no knowledge of good or evil or basically they did not see fault nor had any thought of wrong.

Now days this reality is hard for us to comprehend because humanity's perspective is jam-packed with the knowledge of good and evil. Adam and Eve didn't have this knowledge until the carnal mind came into play in Genesis 3:11. Carnality was the who that told Adam he was naked. So, when we look back into what the garden really was like, we have to remove from our concept the knowledge of good and evil to understand the reality they lived in.

Sin nature and carnal perspective was not present in the garden. If it was then it could not be called Paradise. So, what happened was that when Satan walked into the garden sin came with him. We have to see the two natures that are conflicting in this story. Before the garden encounter, Satan strove to become God and was cast out of heaven and he lost his God-given nature. That is why you won't find the fruit of the Spirit in him. Instead there is fear, anger, hate, and murder coming from the nature of Satan which is sin's root.

When Adam and Eve fell it was because they disobeyed God, which had not been in their nature. Adam and Eve were totally unaware of what the dysfunction of sin was so they had no reason to have their guard up because everything was fine without the need to question. But, then the serpent came into the picture and twisted Gods words. Satan knew he could take advantage of them by introducing something they had never encountered; the idea they were missing something and choosing to question God about their being made in His image.

For God does know that in the day ye eat therefore, then your eyes shall be opened, and ye shall be as gods, knowing good and evil." Genesis 3:5 (KJV).

Note: Satan's tricks haven't changed. He tried the same thing with Jesus in the desert, trying to get Jesus to question His identity as a Son by saying IF YOU are the son of God. (Matthew 4:1-11).

This tells us that Adam and Eve did not know what was evil or good. All they knew was what God had said and they desired to obey Him. They didn't see anything wrong with being like God because they truly loved God and they didn't understand what wrong was.

God knew what had happened and asked Adam, who was hiding in the bushes, "Who told you that you were naked?" In other words, someone else had introduced that word to him because it did not exist in their world because they were made perfect. They hid their nakedness after they came into agreement with Satan's lie about their identity.

What was their nakedness? We think of them having no clothes on. But, was that what it was? No. They had been made in God's image which is spirit. In other words, their spirit hosted their body, they were covered with their spirit man. When they ate the forbidden fruit their spirit man died and their flesh man came alive. Now they were ruled by the flesh. With the spirit's covering gone they were left naked.

God was not mortified by Adams nakedness. God did not hide his eyes from their nakedness. Adam and Eve were now seeing from a natural perspective instead of a spiritual one so they hid. They went from seeing through God's eyes one minute, to seeing from Satan's eyes the next. They now felt what Satan had been feeling this entire time, SHAME! Having now adopted the sin nature of Satan, taking his image, he became their father.

Ye are of your Father the devil, and the lusts of your father ye will do. He was a murderer from the beginning, and abode not in the truth, because there is no truth in him. He speaketh a lie, and the father of it." John 8:34 (KJV).

13

It was through first Adam, sin entered the world, and death by sin; and so, death passed unto all men for all have sinned. (Romans 5:12). Every human born on earth received Adam's sin nature and became the image of fallen Adam.

Even though Jesus put sin to death it is important that we understand what sin is. Adam and Eve began to walk according to the flesh (sin nature) after they lived in the spirit with God. It was a new nature that they put on.

Note: There are two types of flesh that are talked about in scripture. The first is the actual physical skin and bones. The second is the carnal, fleshly, sin nature of man. It's important we identify this so we don't misinterpret what scripture is saying concerning the flesh.

Sin was not in Jesus. This states that, sin was not on the inside of Him, (1 John 3:5) or that He didn't have sin (Hebrews 4:15). What this means is that mankind had something Jesus did not have. SIN. Why did Jesus die for us? It's not just to get us into heaven, like some often teach. But, instead it is to reconnect us to the Father and to abide with Him in heaven as on earth. However, we need to understand that relationship through Christ Jesus is the key. What is it that kept us from the Father? It was what was inside of us.

Jesus came to change our nature back to sons of God and He destroyed the sin nature of the devil in us.

> *He that commits sin is of the devil; for the devil sinned from the beginning. For this purpose, the Son of God was manifested, that he might destroy the works of the devil. 1 John 3:8.*

We need to understand that Satan's seed is dead and its work in our life is a dead reality.

> *Whosoever is born of God doth not commit sin; for HIS SEED remains in HIM..." 1 John 3:9 (KJV).*

This talks about the seed. The seed of Christ has been placed in you and this is why you are born again. The devil had planted his own seed within mankind but Jesus came to rip it out of every single person. The devil's seed functions carnally by nature but we now have a choice to put it off.

Our identity is in Christ and His kingdom realities! No longer is our identity in Adam and in the sin nature's perspective! Thinking this way is how you can turn every mental attack of the enemy into a blessing.

I want to give you a few small steps that will help you grow quickly. It is so good you won't be able to handle the awesomeness Christ Jesus shows toward you every day.

- Understand the currency of heaven is promises. And you have so many of them. Even in areas that you feel are empty they are really full of promises.
- Understand that when you are in Christ, all your circumstances are in Christ as well. That means your problems are in Christ too.
- Understand that everything about you is wrapped in Christ. Now that's out of the way, let's begin.

When you really believe your true identity is in Christ Jesus then you are never challenged by what the enemy is doing, you are only challenged by who God is for you in every situation and who you can become in the midst of every attack of the enemy. You see, without problems you cannot grow in the understanding of who you are in the faith of the Son of God. What if we understood the truth that when we are dead to the old man and alive to Christ Jesus as a new man and that we can learn to rise above every issue and circumstance in our lives? The old man's perspective is constantly being tormented by what the devil is doing because that's all he sees and his life operates in the nature of its father, the devil. But you are not to live life out of your old reality.

> *For they that are after the flesh do mind the things of the flesh; but they that are after the Spirit the things of the Spirit. Romans 8: 5.*

This means we focus our attention onto who we are in the Spirit of Christ, aligning our spirit, soul and body, and what God is doing, not to what the flesh and the enemy are doing. Satan will always try to use our minds to divide us from our union and value as sons of God.

> *For to be carnally minded is death; but to be spiritually minded is life and peace. Because the carnal mind is enmity against God: for it is not subject to the law of God, neither indeed can be. So, then they that are in the flesh cannot please God. But ye are not in the flesh, but in the Spirit, if so be that the Spirit of God dwell in you. Now if any man have not the Spirit of Christ, he is none of his.* (NOT BORN AGAIN). *And if Christ be in you, the body is dead because of sin; but the Spirit is life because of righteousness.* (BEING BORN AGAIN)" *Romans 8:5-10.*

The old man has a "rescue me" mentality because he doesn't understand that he has already been completely rescued. The new man has everything he needs because His source is the Father and He has it all. Whenever the old man gets into arguments with people it is because he is giving into his old way of doing things. He doesn't have anything to rely on but himself. But the new man really doesn't have an anger problem, he has a joy problem. He doesn't understand that right now joy lives in his new heart and that he has all the fruits of the spirit within him. The only issue our ego side has is not knowing how to draw from this fruit because the old man is well practiced in his old ways and habits to solve problems.

In other words, the born-again believer doesn't have a sin issue he has a sin habit. He needs to learn Christ like habits that lineup with his new identity. We now have the divine nature of God living on the inside of us.

> *Grace and peace be multiplied unto you through the knowledge of God, and of Jesus our Lord, according as his divine power hath given unto us all things that [pertain] unto life and godliness, through the knowledge of him that hath called us to glory and virtue: Whereby are given unto us exceeding great and precious promises: that by these ye might be partakers of the divine nature, having escaped the corruption that is in the world through lust."* 2 Peter 1:3-4.*

Your new nature doesn't have issues, only promises. Maybe the problem isn't the problem. What if the problem is that you're trying to solve them out of the egoic self who has to rely on his own ability to fix things instead of relying on God who has placed Christ within you? So, now it's not about God doing something but it's about us becoming a spirit led son in the midst of every natural issue.

Maybe the problem is our perception of the problem? So how we deal with these attacks of the enemy is through our recognizing it for what it is. When you're facing a situation, you can allow it to build you up in Christ and launch you into your identity as it brings you through into victory. So maybe what we should be doing is allowing every situation to sharpen us in Christ. It's not only about what God has called you to do, but its more about who He wants you to be. Every situation brings you closer to Christ because He is all about relationship. He basically is saying, stand close to Me, hold My hand and don't panic! I GOT THIS!

Stop talking about what the enemy is doing and start talking about what God has already done and continues to do in your life. Start to see every situation as an opportunity to grow closer to the mind of God. You will always be faced with problems, but the question is who will your ego become in the midst of them? You will deal with the devil on every level that you're on. You can grow in every situation. But if you are living from your ego the enemy will beat you down to a pulp. He tricks your natural mind to think carnally like him and it catches you up in the chaos of your surrounding world which pulls you out of your position in Christ Jesus. Don't let the enemy or the world around you rob you of your identity in Christ.

Try listening to yourself talk and then ask yourself who is talking right now? Is this the old me or the new me talking? The new you only sees victory because you are seated with a victorious Christ. You have a new way of seeing as well. You have a new way of thinking and speaking and walking. You should be handling everything from the new nature of Christ Jesus. The old you is dead, you are new in Christ Jesus. It's time to start learning to function out of that new you.

I have traveled throughout the world and the issue is the same everywhere I go. People are trying to serve God out of the old man or their egoic realities. Too many churches are pastoring corpses and then wondering why nothing is changing. People are told, "Just try harder. You can do it. Hang in there". NO! Don't hang in there just learn to unite your egoic mind into Christ Jesus realities.

We are to put off the old and put on the new. (Ephesians 4:17-32). God is not merely trying to change you because he has already removed the old you and has given you a recreated life. God did not want to just fix you. He wanted to completely remove the old sin nature in you. The old nature of Adam wasn't just a spiritual issue, it was also the habits that we learned from him that are still lingering, which is why we must renew our minds. That isn't us anymore. Step into your new you.

Some of us have a hard time believing this good news and that is why some backslide. We feel we can never get it right! It's not about arriving but who you become along the way. It's the hope of Glory that is inside of you that does it. It's an inside job. It starts by understanding you are already made right with God even before you can walk it out.

Let's begin to deal with our various problems out of this new mindset. We have to replace one mindset with a different mindset! We can say, "This used to be me! But NOW this is who I am!" It all comes from the new you in Christ. This is the baby stage of Christianity 101. If we don't get this activated in our life we will be serving God out of the wrong identity and all we will get are struggles and issues because the old man is not wired to relate to life in the spirit.

If what you believe to be truth isn't giving you freedom then it's not really truth. Sometimes we cry out for God to move mightily in His power and change us. The truth is that God has already changed us! And we need to understand that God changes us through a process and that he positions us to walk as the new man instead of living from our egoic realities. So, the answer is in the new man who understands his position in Christ and that he can bring heaven to earth through his identity. Even after Christ made us a new man we still function out of the "woe is me" identity (the old man and habits) and we feel as if God didn't come through for us. The good news is that He has already shown up for us every time because He has forever appeared on the inside of us. So, He shows up when we show up in agreement with Him. There are times, as we are growing in our identity in Christ, He will still show up out of His love and grace that is on our life. I can hear God saying, "I have positioned you in every situation to grow and learn but you think it's an attack from the enemy but I'm actually trying to teach you something through it."

Often, we ask God to grow us by asking for more faith. But, God knows you grow into the faith of Jesus within you, as you experience life's issues. So, you need to function from the new man who knows this reality and he takes advantage of every situation that is thrown at him.

What if God is positioning you in every circumstance to walk out your identity in Him? The Holy Spirit is trying to teach you something. But he only teaches the new you because he had to get rid of the old nature and its realities in you so you could walk it out. The understanding of why God only deals with the new man is seen through the wineskin.

Any winemaker, of yesteryear, knew they could not pour new wine into an old wine skin because the changes of the new wine during fermentation would put too much pressure on the old. The old wineskin would break and the new wine would be wasted. So, also God knows not to pour His new into the old. He refuses to waste anything or anyone.

Our core identity is a new man with a new nature and the mindset of the Father.

What All Did Jesus Do?

In this section we ask ourselves: How was Jesus able to do everything and never lack anything? The answer is that He fully understood He had His Father's image, spirit and nature. He, as a Son, had His divine origin from the Father.

Jesus had a heavenly image that is without sin containing the seed of heaven. In this form Jesus did not have a sin nature. But, to save mankind, Jesus put on an image that wasn't His own in order to undo that sin nature. He needed to retrace Adam's steps and not give in to the same lie that established sin. He Himself likewise shared the same humanity so that through death He might break the power of the one who had the power of death (that is, the devil). (Hebrews 2:14). The only way to break the power of death was to share the humanity of man by putting on his body.

By His becoming one of us He then identified with us as the last Adam:

> *For we have not a high priest which cannot be touched with feeling of our infirmities: but was in all points tempted like we are, yet without sin. Hebrews 4:15.*

The key here is that He went through temptation as a man...yet without sin. What Jesus did wasn't as God but as a man who was tempted in every way that we are. He had to overcome as a man, not as God. It was man who came into agreement with Satan and stepped into the sin nature; so, a man had to break that agreement. He became sin to take away our sins, and He did it with no sin. (1 John 3:5).

Here is an important key that we can't miss: Jesus was faithful over His house as a Son. (Hebrews 3:5-6). He was faithful to not please His flesh but only did what the Father was doing and saying. (Romans 15:3; John 6:38). Resolutely, through Holy Spirit upon Him, He governed His flesh. By doing so He showed us that if we hold firmly to our confidence and hope in Christ then we can do all that Jesus did. (Hebrews 10:35-36). We too can walk in the power of Holy Spirit only doing and saying what our Father is saying.

So, what happened during your salvation experience is identical to the encounter Mary had with the Holy Spirit. Our roles as humans became reversed because of what Jesus did. Just as Holy Spirit impregnated the flesh of Mary with heavenly seed, making a gateway into humanity for Jesus, so also, we now have received this same heavenly seed and have been recreated as a new man. We now have the image and nature of Jesus; He transformed us into the origin of the divine Godhead.

Scripture says that Jesus grew in favor. This may seem weird; however, it is because Jesus was an egoic man like us in relationship with the Father. Jesus had the nature of the Father in Him conceived from birth by the Holy Spirit but yet Jesus had the same birth experience we have when we are born from Adam's birth.

So, it was in His nature which made Jesus in the likeness of His Father and one with Him. But Jesus in flesh (as man) grew in favor with God and man.

> *"And Jesus kept increasing in wisdom and stature, and in favor with God and men." Luke 2:52.*

> *"By these He has given us very great and precious promises, so that through them you may share in the divine nature, escaping the corruption that is in the world because of evil desires." 2 Peter 1:4.*

As Jesus grew in favor with God and man, He learned where He was from and who His Father was. He learned that they were one. This brought a sense of security to Jesus. He knew that all of heaven was drawn to Him because He was settled in who He was in the Father.

This brings us into divine oneness with the Father and just like Jesus, we must grow. So, the question is what are we growing in?

Jesus lacked nothing. But how is that so? It is because His Father's nature in Him was not lacking. The same thing happens to us at our born-again experience. The only area we ever lack in is when we operate from our natural mind instead of the mind of Christ. But in actuality, the Spirit has already given us everything, uniting with us to recreate our spirit, soul and body into one new man in Christ Jesus. We must take on the mind of Christ Jesus. (Philippians 2:5).

How Do We Need to Grow?

We learn to grow in the understanding of what we have in the image and likeness of the Father's nature through the Spirit. Then we learn to walk it out just like Jesus.

Jesus, as the Son of God, did not waver or question God. He simply learned everything about His Father; His origin, nature, and function from who He was. He was one with His Father.

> *"For our citizenship is in heaven; from which also we look for the Savior, the Lord Jesus Christ." Philippians 3:20.*

What is revealed in this scripture must become more to us than something we receive when we pass away and go to the Father. It must become more real to us than our earthly citizenship.

We must come to a place where we see ourselves living from the nature and origin of the Father, like Jesus did, who role modeled sonship. We can never come to a place of fully understanding our identity without understanding who Christ is.

This truth must become a reality to us. When we are born-again we receive a heavenly citizenship and the divine nature of the Godhead. We become like Jesus, who is like God. We are born from above. The seed in us is the same seed of Holy Spirit when Jesus was conceived within Mary. This is what happened at our born-again experience.

Jesus was born from the seed of His Father's divine image and likeness in Spirit and nature. At our born-again experience, we too are made in the likeness and image of Jesus in the Father's nature and origin. God's heavenly seed is in us.

We are born of God not of the world. Jesus' Father is now our Father. That's why Jesus calls us His brothers because He knows the same power and authority that resides in Him dwells in us also through Holy Spirit.

See, it is our Father's desire that we have the same mind that was in

Christ Jesus. It's His desire that we learn to think from our heavenly nature and divine origin. He wants us to grow into the full stature of Who Jesus is. Now, that is favor.

We need to take on this mindset: "I am born from above in the Father's image and likeness. My operating manual comes from the Holy Spirit, I function from Him. I do what He says I should do, my ears are turned toward Him and nothing this world says will shake that mindset."

If we are looking at things from an egotistical point-of-view, we are not seeing ourselves like God sees us, as spiritual sons born of Spirit.

> "Therefore, from now on, we regard no one according to the flesh. Even though we have known Christ according to the flesh, yet now we know Him thus no longer. Therefore, if anyone is in Christ, he is a new creation; old things have passed away; behold, all things have become new." 2 Corinthians 5:16-17.

By being in Christ and having his mind we get everything outlined in the following scriptures:

Mind of Christ in... ME

Son

Deliverance is in Me
Dominion is in Me
Power is in Me
Spirit is in Me
Healing is in Me
Victory is in Me
Glory is in Me

Spirit   Nature

God

"His divine power has given us everything we need for life and godliness through the knowledge of Him who called us by His own glory and excellence. "Through these He has given us His precious and magnificent promises, so that through them you may become partakers of the divine nature, now that you have escaped the corruption in the world caused by evil desires." 2 Peter 1:3-4.

"For God wanted them to know that the riches and glory of Christ are for you Gentiles, too. And this is the secret: Christ lives in you. This gives you assurance of sharing his glory." Colossians 1:27 (NLT).

"And I will give you a new heart, and I will put a new spirit in you. I will take out your stony, stubborn heart and give you a tender, responsive heart." Ezekiel 36:26 (NLT).

The answer is in us. We are who God is, through Christ, as a son of God, in the nature of the Father. We carry in us the answer that the world is looking for. So, let His mind be in us with the ability to think as the Father thinks.

Without the mindset of the Father, we will find ourselves thinking like the soul/flesh; taking on fleshly soulish habits and thinking carnally. We will find ourselves questioning the Father when we are living in the flesh like the world does.

The world is controlled by the carnal mind with its fleshly desires and the five senses (touch, taste, hear, smell and sight) when they aren't in unity with the Spirit of God. Our senses and desires aren't bad when we align them to who we are in Christ Jesus.

We can grow up into maturity when we begin to function as free sons of God and embrace His nature in us.

Jesus Governed His Flesh

When the five senses are not controlled by a renewed mind in Christ, they can create a false reality, causing us to question the truth of the Father and His divine nature.

Not only did Jesus hold onto His Father's divine nature but He took authority over His human fleshly nature. (John 17:2). He did not allow it to control Him but He governed it.

Believe it or not Jesus had to deal with His flesh. So, He knows exactly what we all deal with day in and day out. Hebrews 4:15 says, *For we do not have a high priest who is unable to sympathize with our weaknesses, but one who in every respect has been tempted as we are, yet without sin.* (ESV). The big difference between His being tempted and ours is that He did not sin. In other words, He governed His flesh by saying no to it and saying yes to His God nature. (Hebrews 2:17,18).

This is how He overcame for us, He did not give in to the flesh. He did for us what we could not do for ourselves thus making us a new creation into a sinless nature. If Jesus did it then so can we. If we can't wrap our mind around this then our belief system will cause us to live below our created value.

Now, we have the ability to live from heaven on earth and living from our divine nature in the natural realm.

The Kingdom of God is in us (Luke 17:21). What we see in the heavenly celestial (spiritual) realm must become more real to us than the earthly terrestrial realm. We need to go beyond any present belief system that keeps us from having Jesus' mindset.

CHAPTER THREE

IMPORTANCE OF THOUGHT

Father's Thoughts

Thinking like the Spirit of God is a discovery process.

> *"Now the Lord is the Spirit, and where the Spirit of the Lord is, there is freedom. And we all, with unveiled face, beholding the glory of the Lord, are being transformed into the same image from one degree of glory to another. For this comes from the Lord who is the Spirit."* 2 Corinthians 3:17-18.

The Spirit unveils things previously unknown and, in this case, it is the thoughts of who the Spirit is and who the Father is. God is Spirit, a divine being who has a nature that all of the characteristics of the Spirit flows from.

Knowing this will help reveal the Father and how He thinks. In order to learn to think like the Father, we must capture Him in His true identity, in the Spirit and in His nature and likeness.

Some of us have days we feel full of supernatural faith, but the following day we could be down in the dumps of worry and fear. We all know this feeling very well.

We may find ourselves always asking, "Why can't I just be stable in my heart, settled in who the Father is in me, for me and through me all the time?"

After all, we are spirit sons of the living God. We have been filled up with the fullness of the Father's divine nature; having nothing lacking or missing; knowing we are one in Spirit with the Father and Jesus. It is crucial that we know we have the mind of Christ, sanctified, righteous and holy.

This "knowing" has to be more than just head knowledge with a book and words. This knowledge needs to become alive, real to us. It's a shift from the *logos* knowledge into *rhema* knowledge where we walk out what we know and experience the Spirit. This kind of knowledge produces a belief in us that settles us in who we are in the Spirit of Christ Jesus.

What is the big deal about why we should think this way?

In my personal experience, as my mind momentarily pondered on these thoughts, I heard the Spirit begin to teach me saying, "You're not thinking like My Spirit. You need to allow My Spirit to teach you to think like Me."

Instantly, I understood what the Spirit was showing me. I then realized that I had been viewing things from a different perspective.

What is this other perspective? It is carnal, worldly, sensual and fleshly. The flesh has its own perspective just as the Spirit has its perspective.

Unless we are looking through the correct lens, we will see things from the wrong perspective. An example of looking at this through the wrong (or carnal) soul lens is trying to comprehend things from a logical and rational position instead of from the Spirit of God's perspective.

Back to my personal experience: When I tried looking at it from the un-renewed worldly thinking that's rooted in the flesh, I was using the five senses that can only see and communicate through the soul's reality; what it can touch, smell, taste, hear and see.

In other words, I was trying to communicate with God, who is Spirit, from my egoic mindset, logic and rational mind, which portrays a false reality.

In order to change in this area of my life, I knew the key was in making a conscious decision to shift my thought patterns from logic (what makes sense) and to unite my natural reality to function in unity with the Spirit. I had to train my mind to begin to think like the Spirit of the Father!

Really, how is this even possible? You may be pondering, "To think like the Father? Are we really able to do this? Isn't this wrong?"

Listen, before I was married to my wife, Stellah, I used to think I was a failure. I would look at my background, my children and my prior marriage and feel like I had failed. This is because I was looking at it based on my experience and how I reacted to them carnally.

However, if I was to look at it with spiritual lenses, I would have seen all the good things He was seeing in me, including who I am, all my blessings and everything the Spirit has to teach me that comes with my inheritance.

I think I would have never comprehended this back then, but when I fell in love with God, He became my addiction. As a result of falling in love with God, He brought a good woman into my life just to show me that my circumstances do not determine my blessing. I am who God says I am! This taught me a lot about my identity.

My identification card in the supernatural as a son of God is the fact that my body is the dwelling place of the Spirit and the nature of the living God.

In Genesis, God tells us that all of His creation is good. It is important that we understand the body and mind were created by God and that they are good.

So then, what makes the body and mind come into enmity against God?

It's the carnality of the soul; the mind that has given itself over to carnal realities. Your natural mind isn't the problem; the problem is when the dead old carnal man perspectives govern the mind. A mind that is set on the spirit is called the mind of the spirit. This mind communicates and thinks differently than the spirit in us. The egoic mind talks and speaks through our lives and originates from the unrenewed soul that is governed by the five senses. Our five senses aren't bad. They were given to us, even as spirit beings, to reach out to a natural world and encounter Him through it.

Renewing the mind after our born-again experience comes through a lifestyle. This is learning to exercise our senses after the realities of the spirit and bringing the five senses under subjection of the new-man.

That means all challenges, trials, fights and emotions you will have, you will need to know in which mindset you are handling them. Is it from a renewed mind or carnal mind?

Note: When you are in Christ, even your issues are in Him. You cannot separate your situation from who Christ is in you.

The key is to train the mind that the flesh is no longer governing us, but the Spirit, who quickens us into the divine likeness of spirit living and molding who we really are in the Father through Christ Jesus. Then the Spirit will begin governing our soul realities.

The weird part of all this is that the Spirit of Jesus in us (the new us) is functioning from the body. A majority of sons of God struggle because of false mindsets that do not function after the mind of Christ. A mind that is not set on the things that are of the Spirit of God is an un-renewed mind and the voice we hear from that un-renewed mind is what scripture calls the strangers voice.

Renewing the mind is discovering who God truly is for us, through us, and in us in nature and letting the Spirit of God teach us how to take what we learn and walk it out as a lifestyle.

Here's a passage that comes to mind:

> But just as it is written, things which eye has not seen and ear has not heard, and which have not entered the heart of man, all that God has prepared for those who love Him. For to us God revealed them through the Spirit; for the Spirit searches all things, even the depths of God. 1 Corinthians 2:9-10.

At times we have been told not to go too deep or that is not for us to know, but the scripture says that our teacher, the Holy Spirit, searches out the deep things of God.

Jesus said:

> *"Ask and it will be given to you; seek and you will find; knock and the door will be opened to you. Matthew 7:7.*
>
> *Until now you have not asked for anything in My name. Ask and you will receive, so that your joy may be complete. John 16:24.*

We unknowingly have been taught not to ask questions. But if Jesus tells us to ask and the Spirit who knows the Father lets us know that it is okay to ask Holy Spirit anything, then we should ask.

For who among men knows the thoughts of a man except the spirit of the man which is in him? (1 Corinthians 2:11) Even the thoughts of God no one knows except the Spirit of God that's in you, giving you the ability to think like God in Christ.

> *Now we have received, not the spirit of the world, but the Spirit who is from God, so that we may know the things freely given to us by God, which things we also speak not in words taught by human wisdom, but in those taught by the Spirit, combining spiritual thoughts with spiritual words. But a natural man (flesh) does not accept the things of the Spirit of God, for they are foolishness to him; and he cannot understand them, because they are spiritually appraised. But he who is spiritual appraises all things, yet he himself is appraised by no one. For who has known the mind of the Lord, that he will instruct Him. But, we have the mind of Christ." 1 Corinthians 2:12-16.*
>
> *"...and that you be renewed in the spirit of your mind, and put on the new self, which in the likeness of God has been created in righteousness and holiness of the truth." Ephesians 4:23-24.*

"Have this attitude [or mind] in yourselves which was also in Christ Jesus." Ephesians 2:5.

"As for you, the anointing which you received from Him abides in you, and you have no need for anyone to teach you; but as His anointing teaches you about all things, and is true and is not a lie, and just as it has taught you, you abide in Him." 1 John 2:27.

We are told in Romans, *...do not be conformed to this world,* to the standards of the world, *but be transformed by the renewing of your mind, so that you may prove what the will of God is, that which is good and acceptable and perfect."* (Romans 12:2). This renewed mind will cause us to be transformed.

It would seem then that it is God's very purpose that we think like Him. Thinking like Him proves His good, acceptable and perfect will of his Son, Jesus Christ in us the hope of glory!

How Do We Think Like Holy Spirit?

I am convinced that the mind of Christ thinks from the divine nature in the likeness of the Spirit of God. The mind of Christ does not think like the un-renewed soulish mind. Why? Because it is not affected by logic and the five senses which are controlled by the carnality of the world, the terrestrial realm.

Now your senses and feelings, logic and rationale aren't bad, it's when carnality governs them. With self-control from the Spirit, one can govern themselves to walk in the Spirit of God by controlling their feelings and emotions into the right thinking in God.

"All of us used to live that way, following the passionate desires and inclinations of our sinful nature. By our very nature, we were subject to God's anger, just like everyone else." Ephesians 4:23.

"For to be carnally minded is death; but to be spiritually minded is life and peace." Romans 8:6.

32

Note: In the natural we are told not to trust our emotions and feelings. I believe our five senses, feeling and emotions, that are governed by the Spirit of God can be trusted.

Jesus said that His words are spirit and life which is where thinking in the mind of the Spirit is derived from.

> *"It is the Spirit who gives life; the flesh is no help at all.*
> *The words that I have spoken to you are spirit and life."*
> *John 6:63.*

The mind of Jesus, the will of God, is contained in the written (logos) word and in the Spirit (rhema) that brings life to the word. (Hebrews 4:12).

Obviously, God's thoughts are limitless. Therefore, our thoughts are limitless as sons of God. Thereby, believing in God's specific ways and thinking like Him we can then-

> *"Be imitators of God, therefore, as dearly loved children."*
> *Ephesians 5:1.*

When our mind is renewed to align with the Spirit of God then our thoughts will be filled with the life and the fullness of the Godhead. We then through Holy Spirit have a direct line into Father God's thoughts and ways. It's a win, win for sure.

It is Finished

When Jesus was on the cross He stated that it was finished. There are speculations as to exactly what He was referring to. The Old Covenant? The work of redeeming mankind? Possibly it could be lots of other things that we haven't seen yet.

So, what was finished? I think it was the completion of God seeking out and saving those who were lost and sins atonement given so men would be reconciled back unto God. (Luke 19:10).

Personally, I think one thought behind Jesus' words," It is finished.",
is how He intended us to respond when told to believe that we have
received when we pray.

> "*So, Jesus answered and said to them, 'Have faith in God.*
> *For assuredly, I say to you, whoever says to this mountain,*
> *'Be removed and be cast into the sea,' and does not doubt in*
> *his heart, but believes that those things he says will be done,*
> *he will have whatever he says. Therefore, I say to you,*
> *whatever things you ask when you pray, believe that you*
> *receive them, and you will have them." Mark 11:22-24.*

I believe He is teaching us how the Spirit of the Father's faith works,
just like the Father has the ability to call the end from the beginning.

The Bible teaches Faith is a person. It tells us that the faith of the
Son of God is a gift of the Spirit meaning, Faith comes from the
Spirit of God living in you.

> "*Looking unto Jesus the author and finisher of our faith;*
> *who for the joy that was set before Him endured the cross,*
> *despising the shame, and is set down at the right hand of the*
> *throne of God." Hebrews 12:2.*

When we believe like Jesus, then what we say will happen and we
should not doubt in our heart. In other words, when we speak "it is
finished" it is the same as what Jesus did on the cross.

> "*You will also declare a thing, and it will be established for*
> *you." Job 22:28.*

The Bible does not say it might be established, but it will be
established! God calls the end from the beginning. This is faith, the
power of "it is finished;" seeing the end from the beginning.

Jesus while on the cross spoke in agreement when He said, it is
finished. He settled what the Father spoke about from the
foundations of the world. It is finished is a prophetic declaration in
agreement with the image and likeness of the Spirit of the Father in
us.

The Spirit of God thinks powerfully and we are told to think this way as well. However, this requires a complete shift of gears in our minds from carnal, soulish, fleshly thinking to the Spirit's way of thinking. This is rooted deeply in our core identity as sons of God.

If we entwine these thoughts from time to time, reverting to unbelief and doubt, when circumstances don't change immediately, we become what James describes as double-minded. James 1:6-7 says that one, ...*must ask in faith without any doubting, for the one who doubts is like the surf of the sea, driven and tossed by the wind. For that man ought not to expect that he will receive anything from the Lord being a double-minded man, unstable in all his ways.*

So, then what is a double minded man? It's the reality of the soulish man versus the reality of the spirit man. They become tossed about between two opinions which make them unstable in all their ways and not to expect to receive anything from the Lord!

So, why is it so hard to not be double-minded? It's because the carnality that governs the soul has created a false reality. That reality causes us to trust in the carnal mind rather than the mind of the Spirit.

Having a double mind keeps us from engaging in the "it is finished" reality. A double mind is wrapped up in doubt and fear. We are called to a higher place of understanding where all doubt is removed from the doomed funnel that drains all hope and trust. Calling a halt to the double mind launches us into our knowing without a doubt the reality of "it's finished" in God.

God is Love

I want to point out a key truth you need as you learn to walk as a new man. It's that God doesn't have love, He is Love! Love is the fruit of the person in Spirit. Therefore, His thoughts are thoughts of love. So, the Spirit is the root of love. Walk in the Spirit and love will manifest. Our spirit man has the love of God because it is of Him.

1 Corinthians 13 tells us that it doesn't matter what we do, or don't do because without love, it means nothing. In other words, legalism (law of sin and death) or the old-man's nature has been superseded by the spirit of love.

The old man (first Adam), has been replaced by the new-man (second Adam), the life-giving Spirit of Jesus' love in us which is the nature of the spirit.

Faith (Jesus) works by love (The Spirit of the Father's Nature). That's why faith (Jesus) chooses to believe in His own word even if we don't understand it fully because of the motives of the person, Faith (Jesus), makes stuff come to pass. God's Spirit is love-therefore faith works by the Spirit of God in Christ Jesus!

The Spirit of God which is the Fathers thoughts are love thoughts. So, if we are to think like Him, our thoughts will flow from our God nature, producing thoughts of love also.

> *"Through these He has given us His precious and magnificent promises, so that through them you may become partakers of the divine nature, now that you have escaped the corruption in the world caused by evil desires." 2 Peter 1:4.*

Mediate on the following scripture for it describes love precisely:

> *"Love is patient, love is kind and is not jealous; love does not brag and is not arrogant, does not act unbecomingly; it does not seek its own, is not provoked, does not take into account a wrong suffered, does not rejoice in unrighteousness, but rejoices with the truth; bears all thing, believes all things, hopes all things, endures all things. Love never fails..." 1 Corinthians 13:4-8.*

This portion of scripture is describing the Father's nature in us. This allows us to get to know the Father and His heart toward us. This also allows us to know the difference between the strangers' voice and the voice of the Spirit of love. In return, knowing the Father's voice helps us know who we are as Spirit sons and our divine nature. Now our spirit knows that we are one with the spirit of love filled completely with all the fullness of His love! Who is love? It's a person, Father God! He is Spirit and the root of love.

Believe and proclaim it as an agreement over your life. Think like God thinks! Think Love!

Begin to study scripture looking at the words love, grace, peace, power, authority, faith, and hope as a person. Learn to read scripture as a living and active person.

> *For the word of God is living and active, sharper than any two-edged sword, piercing to the division of soul and of spirit, of joints and of marrow, and discerning the thoughts and intentions of the heart. Hebrews 4:12.*

> *Now faith is a substance of the things hoped for and the evidence of things not seen. Hebrews 11:1.*

Scripture says Jesus is the image of the invisible God. Hebrews 12:2 says, Jesus is the author of faith, so if faith is a person when you read the Hebrews 11:1 again in context it will read like this: *Now Faith (Jesus) is the substance of things hoped for and evidence of things not seen.*

Coming into our spiritual sonship (our new man) we begin to know and believe the love God has for us. After all, God is love, and he who abides in love abides in God, and God in him.

CHAPTER FOUR

RENEWED THINKING

Head Games

The Word of God has many verses about the mind of the natural man. In many cases, the mind is literally a war zone with thoughts and imaginations blasted into our heads. Many people are at a loss for words and don't know what to do when it comes to dealing with the mind and trying to figure out how to overcome and conquer this perceived giant in our lives.

Man's mind is a beautiful and powerful thing. It can be used to logically think out the construction of a skyscraper and used to invent all kinds of new inventions that benefit mankind. The mind can control man's outlook, the feelings and emotions producing the drive/will in man for either good or bad. The Bible speaks about the "bait" the enemy uses to tempt man. When taking a closer look at these verses it is easy to see temptation centers around mental, sensual, physical and worldly things. I want to show you how Satan's desire is to conquer the mind of sons and daughters of God.

Our minds have the ability to imagine things. The mind is centered on what makes sense to it and what it already knows. If the mind can't logically think something through, it will function from a point of "lack of understanding." Later we will discover how logic in the natural, sensual and worldly system does not think like the mind of Christ.

The Holy Spirit is teaching us, that as we trust in God it moves us away from our own understanding into acknowledging God in all our ways so that He may direct our path.

> *"Trust in the Lord with all your heart and lean not on your own understanding; In all your ways acknowledge Him, And He shall direct your paths." Proverbs 3:5,6.*

Think about this for a second. What this verse is saying is that God will not always make sense to your logical, worldly mindset. Yes, God can relate to us on the logical level for sure, but where we go as we grow in the Spirit, is to a place where God will take our hand and lead us to places that is exceedingly and abundantly above anything we can ever ask or think. (Ephesians 3:20).

You might be asking why? It is because we often measure smartness based on logic or the wisdom we obtained according to the world and logical system. Our minds dictate a major part of how we perceive others, ourselves and how to live life.

Romans 8:5-7 could be explained this way: *For those who live according to the flesh set their minds on the things of the flesh,* (and its realities) *but those who live according to the Spirit, the things of the Spirit of God's* (realities). *For to be carnally minded* (governed by the worldly, fleshly, sensual desires of man) *is death, but to be spiritually minded is life and peace. Because the carnal mind is enmity* (fights) *against God; for it is not subject to* (the love) *the law of God, nor indeed can be. So then, those who are in the flesh* (carnal mindset) *cannot please God. But you are not in the flesh but in the Spirit, if indeed the Spirit of God dwells in you. Now if anyone does not have the Spirit of Christ, he is not His.* (Emphasis mine).

Then, why is the mind waging war against the Spirit of God? Or why is Satan so often targeting our minds and giving us worldly and sensual thoughts?

This is because the mind functions out of what it perceives is true; what it can feel, taste, hear, smell and see. These five senses are the gateway of the enemy to trick us into a false reality through our imaginations.

The fact is truth is not what your mind tells you it is because Truth is a person; He has a name, Jesus. Jesus functions out of a different place and another reality.

He functions from, out of and through the unseen part of us. So, when the mind can't feel, taste, hear, smell and see something it automatically marks it as unreal. But it should be Jesus who defines our reality.

2 Corinthians 10:4 says that the weapons of our warfare are not carnal. So, what does that mean? Let us look at carnality. The definition of carnal is: worldly, fleshly or sensual. So, if carnality is not our weapon, then the question we should ask is whose weapon is it?

Scripture states that the god of this world has blinded the mind of those who do not believe God. When we function out of our carnal mind we are blinded from hearing or receiving God's thoughts. (2 Corinthians 4:4). Most often we do not realize we aren't hearing God.

> *"But He turned and said to Peter, 'Get behind me Satan!'"*
> *Matthew 16:23.*

Jesus refers here to Peter as Satan! Why did Jesus call Peter Satan? It is because Peter was thinking from his natural man and not from God's mindset.

James 3:13-17 talks about ego, self-seeking, boastful, sensual and worldly wisdom, which is referred to as demonic. Take a moment and see how everything mentioned in this scripture has to do with the natural man and how living a life controlled by these things is not of God. Think it out! Pray about it and see what the Holy Spirit shows you.

The god of this world has blinded the unbeliever's minds, preventing them from seeing the illuminating light of the gospel of the glory of Christ. The enemy is actively blinding the minds of people from the image of God.

Colossians 1:21 says that we once were alienated and enemies in our mind through wicked works that were tools for the enemy's use. So, what tool does the enemy use? Our minds.

Satan keeps us in the mind of the flesh which does not submit to God's law and is hostile toward Him. (Romans 8:7). Indeed, the carnal mind cannot submit to God so it's in enmity against God.

In 2 Corinthians 11:3-5 there is something profound revealed here. In most scripture Paul really doesn't mention he fears anything. But in this passage, he said he was afraid that just as the serpent deceived Eve by his cunning and that he will also use our thoughts to lead us astray. He feared that we would get tricked in our minds just as Adam and Eve were tricked into believing they could even question God. Paul didn't want people to be tricked into another Jesus, another spirit or another gospel.

Another important question is to ask ourselves, what is a stronghold? It is when the enemy has created a reality outside of God within the logical mind causing a believer to second guess Him or even worse, to come against His knowledge. What this does is create a perspective that allows a believer's imagination to run wild and build a false reality that appears real and true but yet isn't truth.

In the Garden of Eden, Satan tricked Eve by getting her focused-on knowledge outside of God's. It was through a lie of deception and trickery that Satan bombarded her mind. It is very easy to see how a mind that is set on carnality is Satan's playground.

Think about James 1:14 that states one is tempted when he is drawn away by his own *evil desires* or lust of the flesh. It is important that we notice temptation comes from a mindset of the flesh, carnality, and a world system outside of God. Therefore, in 1 Corinthians 10: 3-4 it says you don't battle against the flesh. Why? Because the flesh is what the enemy uses as bait to tempt God's children away from God. The scripture says walk in the Spirit and you will not carry out the desires (lust) of the flesh.

The bait temptation uses is the carnal flesh, it taps into the sensual part of humanity and uses it to access the mind of man. The number one goal of Satan is to get into your head. If he can govern your mind, he will control the body/flesh and use it to carry out what is demonic, according to James 3:13-17. Let me quickly expose the trickery of the enemy by showing you how he turns fleshly temptation into a conscious mental thought.

Because man is living on the earth we cannot separate temptation from the mind of the believer. Therefore, as a whole man that is spirit, soul and body, it is important for us to learn how to walk in the Spirit so we can have renewed thoughts. Based on Romans 8:6, the key to avoid carnality is the renewing of our natural mind. This is done by keeping certain doors closed so that we don't leave any room for the enemy to trick us in our mind. The key is learning the mind of the Spirit and to live there.

In Christ, we have the power to overthrow the logical wisdom of this world that tries to raise itself above the knowledge of God. One thing we don't realize is that the Spirit of God has a mind too. The scripture tells us that we are to take on His mindset.

> *"Let this mind be in you that was also in Christ."*
> *Philippians 2:5.*

> *"He who searches our heart knows the mind of the Spirit."*
> *Romans 8:27.*

God's passion is that we learn to change our thinking to think like Him in all things. We should live a daily life of repentance. The meaning of repentance is to change one's mind. So, the question is what mind are we renewing it to? It's the Spirit of Christ's mind. Daily our prayer to God should be "Today Lord, my desire is to think like you." Most people don't know they can think like Christ.

As a believer, your spirit is saved and the body and soul have been made complete and whole in Christ. We become the flesh of Christ's flesh and bone of His bone, united in one Spirit with Him. There is however one issue we must deal with, which are the thoughts running through the mind. A mind that hasn't been renewed will have thoughts running wildly unleashed.

For new and as well as seasoned believers, the mind can be a constant war zone. I don't think there is any other place in a believer's life where they are attacked more than their mind. Exposing the enemy's tricks is to know that all his devices and deceptions are in the mind. Notice how Satan did not go after Eve's physical attributes. He went after her mind and from there other issues arose.

There is a basic plan Satan uses to control our mind. It seems to work every time since the fall. It is through the introduction of a seemingly simple thought. The key is what we do with this thought. This is where the enemy's Trojan horse captures our mind.

Let's look at the thought process. First the thought is introduced. This is the crucial stage that will determine its effect on the mind. At this stage it can be accepted or rejected. Stage two is when the thought is pondered upon. As we think on it then it begins to gain complete dominance over us. Then it moves on to the third and final stage where the thought is acted upon. This is where most pondered thoughts, once unseen, become visible.

The process of thought described above works for either good or evil and is determined by whether it is from one's flesh, the enemy or from the spirit man. Paul knew the magnitude of taking the thoughts captive to the obedience of Christ in his warning to the church. (2 Corinthians 10:5). When we learn to govern our thoughts then our minds are becoming renewed into the mind of Christ and we won't fall prey to the trickery of the enemy.

For a progressive renewing of your mind you have to become practiced in governing your thought process so your pattern of thought transforms into the mind of Christ. In other words, it isn't a onetime change of thought but a life-style of establishing God's thoughts.

Another trick of Satan's is to steal, kill and destroy the knowledge of God that we already have. Satan tries to complicate the gospel and get us focused on another spirit and another perspective of Jesus according to 2 Corinthians 11:3-5. The mind is the most vulnerable area for believers if it has not been renewed. Satan focuses on the mind because it is the one place in you that he ruled before your born-again experience. Satan has no power over your spirit in Christ or your new heart. So, he goes after the one place you give him access to because you haven't learned to know who God is for you, in you and through you. That part is defenseless until it is renewed in who it is supposed to be in Christ Jesus.

There is a truth, many don't understand, that a believer has a new spirit, new heart, but a natural mind.

Many believers are confused because they know they are a new creation but can't figure out why they battle thoughts which are opposite the truth of Jesus within them. The war zone is activated when your new heart speaks one way and your natural mind thinks another way. Your spirit knows something, but your mind can't figure it out. While your spirit is speaking the truth to you, your mind is saying that it doesn't make any logical sense.

Most people have great intentions in their hearts but don't have clarity in their minds. While one's motives are good, the mind has its own ideas and a set way it wants to follow. Now can you see why the mind is a fertile ground for the enemy to trick believers?

Life is more important than knowledge. Spiritual knowledge and wisdom is as different as night and day compared to worldly knowledge and wisdom.

Let me ask you a few questions to ponder?

1. Who is in control of your thinking?
2. Do you control your thinking?
3. If you do, then why do you lose control over it?

You have self-control because the Spirit of God's fruit resides within you. Many think God is in control. NO, He isn't in control but He is in charge.

So, if neither Satan nor God controls your thinking, then who does?

Since God gave you self-control in the Spirit, you can control what mind you are in. The enemy can only trick you. Here is a red flag to look for that can signal the appropriate time to renew our minds: *when our mind is screaming out of control.* This is a sign that the enemy is tricking and deceiving us with a false imagination of who God is for us. This is where learning to take our thoughts captive comes into play.

Practical tip: The thoughts that Satan is putting in our heads are usually along the lines where we feel lack, missing something or anything that is contrary to the first thought we had.

Satan can't read our mind but he can play head games with us by prodding our flesh. He will shoot fiery darts at us and see what bait we will swallow. Our fleshly, mental actions and responses give the enemy tips on how he can hook us into his reality and plan. Many times, Christians are playing on Satan's home field and don't even know it. Why? Because their minds haven't been renewed into knowing God's reality and His thoughts.

Why are the sons of God's minds bombarded? It is because they are not changing how they think towards the truth. If the world's truth becomes our reality, then it opens a doorway for the enemy to pummel the bulls eye in our head. Yes, a child of God gets mentally attacked by the enemy when they don't take charge of their thoughts.

Let me share with you a personal experience of a mental attack. Many calls this a spiritual attack, but I want you to think this through and take it to the Holy Spirit who is your teacher.

Some time ago, before I was to leave for a three-week ministry road trip, there was a major flu spreading throughout our community and it was turning into pneumonia for many. Two days before our departure, I started getting flu symptoms. When I feel sickness coming to me, I usually start praising God. So, I did just that. I started praising God and not relying on what I was seeing, but on who He is for me.

However, this did not go as I had hoped. The next day I woke up worse, my lungs were hurting and I was feeling pain in my entire body. Later in the afternoon, one of my wife's friends stopped by and said she needed prayer as she had just come from the hospital and the doctor said she had pneumonia.

So, we prayed for her and my wife, Stellah said· "Paul hasn't been feeling well either." So, they started talking to each other while I listened to their conversation. I could hear my thoughts speaking to me: "Paulyb, remember when you were 14 and you almost died of pneumonia?" I responded with: "I take that thought captive and Father I thank you for keeping me whole." But, the thoughts persisted, "Do you feel that pain in your back? I bet it is pneumonia. You are leaving in a day, what if you go and the pneumonia kicks in?" At this point I felt the fear creeping in. I know how to deal with this by the way, I teach this stuff you know. Right?

I walked back to my bedroom and prayed and talked to God as my mind kept playing games with me. After about 10 minutes of taking my thoughts captive and getting some control over my thoughts, I walked out of the room and Stellah said, as I passed by them, "Honey why don't you go see a doctor please." I quickly said, "No honey I'm ok."

After 20 minutes of listening to them, my mind started racing so I told Stellah we could go to the doctor. As we were pulling up in the parking lot of the doctor's office, I could feel my heart racing.

Now let me give you a quick background story about why my heart was racing. I grew up with my Aunt and Uncle. At that time, my Aunt was studying to become a doctor. So, I can remember as a young boy that when she needed to give me medication, she would say, "if you don't listen to me I'm going to take you to the doctor and they're going to give you a shot with a big needle." I used to watch her study for tests and watch surgeries on TV. Those things stuck in my mind creating a mental battle within me that made me hate going to the doctor even to this day.

As we arrived at the clinic and started walking in, my mind was saying, "What if you have pneumonia? What if they find something else? What if they find a lump in your lung or body?" Crazy mental gymnastics began tumbling around, creating imaginations with all sorts of scenarios. Stellah could see my face turning red and I could feel my heart racing. I couldn't stop pacing. Stellah told me to relax and I asked myself: "What the heck is this? I know who I am; I know how to control myself." But frustrations started setting in because I wasn't controlling my emotions very well.

I was called to the examination room where they checked my blood pressure. It was at 190/100, which is super high. The doctor came in and said he wanted to do an X-ray. My mind was at it again wondering, "what if they find something?" After the X-rays, they told me to give them a few minutes to read the film and instructed us to sit down in the waiting room. My mind went crazy and I got so worked up that I went to the bathroom and threw up.

On returning, I found the doctor waiting and he said "Paulyb, we looked at all the results and we don't see anything wrong with you." Let me tell you that at that moment, every feeling, emotion and imagination I had created in my thoughts was instantly gone. He took my blood pressure again before I left and it had dropped to 139/86. I walked away puzzled.

Wow that was crazy! I told Stellah that it was a mental attack and I was living from a false reality in my mind and believing a lie. Many people would say that it was a spiritual attack, but this was not what it was. It was the simple fact that I was not taking control over my thoughts. It was a mental attack.

Think about it, what is a spiritual attack? Many will say worry, pain, hurt, feelings, and emotions like depression, anxiety and fear. Those are all physical not spiritual.

I'm only sharing this to show you how the enemy attacks our minds and if it's not functioning from a renewed state, it can create a mental mess within us if we allow it, like it did in me. It was a great lesson for me to learn not to jump the gun allowing my mind to think the worst in a situation. It was also a lesson in knowing God is faithful to those whose minds have stayed on Him. (Isaiah 26:3).

The devil can never play games on us if we walk in the Spirit, living in self-control and not giving him a place in our minds. The Spirit of Christ is our leverage. But if we function from our natural man and are being governed by our feelings and emotions then it's the wrong spirit. It can produce a reality in our mind of corrupt thoughts turning it into an imagination that will open the door to a physical and mental stronghold. It's not a spiritual stronghold because Jesus purchased your spirit. But physically and mentally, you can allow the lie to create a false reality that looks true but isn't the truth.

Your mind in the natural is the human mind. If you take ownership of your mind in the Spirit of Christ Jesus and choose not to let it be invaded by any other belief system then the devil has no right over your mind. When he does try to throw a fiery dart at you, you will see it coming. If it hits you, you will say, "No, that's not how the kingdom thinks." Remember you are Jesus's property! The enemy cannot trespass on Jesus' property unless you open the door and you receive him. You have no enemies in the Spirit of God, unless you accept him into the carnal mind that is set on the flesh.

Therefore, renewing the mind is so critical to the body, so that we can learn to think like the Spirit of Jesus in all situations. The enemy will throw darts at us, but when we know our Jesus we will not be tricked as Adam and Eve were into believing a lie.

Even Jesus experienced temptation. In the wilderness, Jesus was tempted to give up, to quit and not go to the cross. He had emotions and feelings speaking to Him too, to the extent that He sweated blood. Let me ask you, when was the last time you were tempted so much that you were sweating blood? Our Savior did experience temptation. His flesh did not want to die and his natural man's will didn't want to go through with the process of the cross. Notice something; this is a physical and mental issue that Jesus was experiencing, not a spiritual one. Why? Because His Spirit belongs to His Father.

But, Jesus at the last minute pulls through. He functions from the Spirit of self-control. Self-control is simply controlling natural man's nature. Jesus says something profound, "Not My will, but your will be done." Who is the first will mentioned here? It's his natural man's will, but Your will be done is referring to God's will. Self has a will and God has a will. The lesson is that self-will gives you a choice to go outside God or to go along with God. Yes, there is a choice but only one counts and at the end of the day, God's will is supreme. Any other will outside of God's is a lie. Jesus through this experience taught us, as sons of God, how we can live from the Spirit while going through physical and mental challenges.

Wrong Thinking

Unfortunately, some Christian circles teach that we can never understand God's ways. This is directly opposite from what the Scriptures tell us. It says that we have the mind of Christ and that wisdom accompanies those who have righteousness through Jesus.

What is really interesting is that some of those false beliefs are wrongly drawn from the passage below. Such as where it says "the eye has not seen" verse. But in that same chapter there are a couple of very big "buts."

> But as it is written: "What no eye has seen, nor ear has heard, and has not entered into heart of man, what God has prepared for those loving Him. For God has revealed it to us through the Spirit. For the Spirit searches all things, even the depths of God. For who among men knows the things of the man, except the spirit of the man within him? So also, no one knows the things of God, except the Spirit of God. Now we have not received the spirit of the world, but the Spirit from God, that we may know the things having been granted to us by God. 1 Corinthians 2:9-12.

Allow verse 12 to settle in your heart. We have been given the Father's Spirit. John 4:24 paints a great picture of the image of God, His image is Spirit. Jesus said in John 14:9, "*Anyone who has seen Me has seen the Father.*" Was Jesus talking about Himself in the flesh or the spirit nature as one in the Father? This revelation will help us see the way God sees.

> Which also we speak, not in words taught of human wisdom, but in those taught of the Spirit, communicating spiritual things by spiritual means. 1 Corinthians 2:13.

We are born again of the Spirit, not of the flesh. The carnal man cannot understand the Spirit in the sons of God. It is the Spirit who teaches us. We glean from man but we always take it to the Holy Spirit who is our teacher.

> *But the natural man does not accept the things of the Spirit of God; for they are foolishness to him, and he is not able to understand them, because spiritually they are discerned. 1 Corinthians 2:14.*

In this verse Apostle Paul speaks of the natural man and the carnal soul, logical and rational mind of non-believers and believers alike who don't know who they are in Spirit and in the nature of the Father.

Even the soul's carnal perspective of man in general affects all of us whether saved or unsaved. If a person is controlled by the flesh and the carnal mind, they will think after the wisdom of the world which is controlling them, be it carnal or Spirit. (James 3:13-17). James says that when someone is governed by the senses of the world and carnality that it is demonic.

> *But he who is spiritual judges all things, but he himself is judged by no one." 1 Corinthians 2:15.*

This is an amazing scripture! As Spirit sons we judge all things, because those who are in Spirit see like the Father and judge in love, grace, mercy, self-control, kindness, patience, etc. The best part is that the sons of God are judged by no one. As a son, God sees that you are like Him, in His image and likeness.

> *For who has known the mind of the Lord? Who will instruct Him?' But we have the mind of Christ." 1 Corinthians 2:16.*

Can God be judged? The answer is No. So, what makes us think we, who are in His image and likeness, can be judged by others? Father God is our only judge and He will judge His children after His Spirit in them.

Too many Christian's have accepted the false idea that the spirit world is bad. Much of the Church has rejected it claiming it is connected with the demonic or New Age. Yes, they function in unexplainable things that are in the spirit realm but it didn't originate with them. They have only hijacked a spiritual truth that began with God. God is Spirit so the spirit world is His.

Once the church begins to function in the reality of God's Spirit realm then we will connect with our heritage given us through Christ Jesus. We will then take our wrong thinking and turn it into right thinking that will plug us into the Spirit of God.

Renewing Your Mind

In a previous chapter, we read about how the Father functions from His nature of love. This not only shows how people are in the Spirit of the Father, but also how the Father is with His people. God doesn't tell us to do one thing while He does another. After all, He is the same yesterday, today and forever. He has never and will never change His mind about you as sons of God.

In the book of Genesis, when God finished creating the earth and humanity, He looked and saw that "everything was good." This is an important key in knowing how God thinks about you and all of the people in the world today. The Father sees us as good.

Philippians 4 summarizes this nicely:

> *Rejoice in the Lord always; again, I will say, rejoice! Let your gentle spirit be known to all men. The Lord is near. Be anxious for nothing, but in everything by prayer and supplication with thanksgiving let your requests be made known to God. And the peace of God, which surpasses all comprehension, will guard your hearts and your minds in Christ Jesus. Finally, brethren, whatever is true, whatever is honorable, whatever is right, whatever is pure, whatever is lovely, whatever is of good repute, if there is any excellence and if anything, worthy of praise, dwell on these things. The things you have learned and received and heard and seen in me practice these things, and the God of peace will be with you." Philippians 4:4-9.*

The Spirit of God thinks good thoughts only. He gives hope; He builds up rather than tearing down. God's desire toward each of us is loveliness, health, wealth, peace, protection, favor and power etc.

Christ living in us with power and authority allows us to face any situation knowing that we are not alone. The thought of that should give us peace and confidence in Who is in us.

Faith comes by hearing and hearing the word of God. This we achieve through reading the word of God and being taught by the Holy Spirit. Also, I believe God's word can supersede the words in the Bible. That means the Word of God will speak to you as well from the Spirit.

The word of God will not profit us anything if we do not allow the Holy Spirit to renew our minds to the truth.

Our minds are renewed with good thoughts when we allow what God says about us to become a reality by living it out. For example, Jesus said that we should not be worried about anything and to not allow stuff to pressure us. Instead, He told us to rejoice at all times, even when we are facing trials, anything less than that is a lie from our soulish carnal mind

However, for it to be effective, we have to renew our soulish mind from our circumstances to who God is for us, in us, and through us. This will happen if we allow the Holy Spirit to remind us of who we are according to the word of God. If we have worry and stress then we are not living from the promises of God, but rather soulish realities. God's purpose for us is that our minds would meditate on who Jesus recreated us to be as sons of the Highest God who is good at all times.

If God bears such good thoughts about us, then it is a given that bad thoughts don't come from the Spirit, they are rooted in the carnality of the mind!

The Spirit of God created the whole universe and then He saw that everything was good! This includes friendship, families, kindness, goodness and all are His creation.

We have been taught that God kills people and destroys things and takes away in order to teach us a lesson. The Bible holds different thoughts:

> *"The thief comes only to steal and kill and destroy; I came that they may have life and have it abundantly [or have abundance]." John 10:10.*

The above scripture is Jesus, pulling no punches, and telling us straight up who is doing what. This is a no-brainer, if it is good; it is the Spirit of God. If it is bad, it is the thief. Who is the thief? It is Satan's thoughts that govern the soul; that create bad thinking.

We are instructed by scripture to *let this mind of the Spirit of Jesus be in you that was in Christ* (Philippians 2:5); knowing the difference between good thoughts and evil thoughts. *If you, knowing how to give good gifts to your children, how much more does our Father in heaven know how to give good gifts to His children.* (Matthew 7:11).

We can choose to live from the carnal mind's way of operating as the judge of good and evil or from our new position in Christ. Rotten seed produces rotten fruit. Righteous seed produces righteous fruit. Nothing good was in us so Jesus came to kill that part of us.

> *Know ye not, that so many of us were baptized into Jesus Christ were baptized into His death? Romans 6:3.*

The keyword here is KNOW YE NOT? Basically, this is asking, "didn't you know this?" You died. The old you, referring to the sin nature, is dead.

> *For ye are dead, and your life is hid with Christ in God. Colossians 3:3 (KJV).*

We must understand that we have died and our life is now hidden in Christ Jesus. This is very important if we are to grow in the Spirit. We must keep our thoughts on the things of the spirit.

For to be carnally minded is death: but to be spiritually minded is life and peace. Romans 8:6.

We are thinking under the old carnal man which is from the fallen nature of Adam. This kind of mindset actually alienates us from God.

And you, who once were alienated and enemies in your mind by wicked works, yet now He has reconciled in the body of His flesh through death, to present you holy, and blameless, and above reproach in His sight. Colossians 1:21-22.

And you, being dead in your sins and the uncircumcised of your flesh, hath He made alive together with Him, having forgiven you all trespasses. Colossians 2:13.

This used to be us, enemies in our own minds. The carnal mind is a big part of the struggle that we have as born-again believers. Why? Because we haven't been fully convinced the flesh is dead and that we can live from the mind of the Spirit in the new man. (Ephesians 2:14-16).

Romans 12:2 tells us to renew the mind *"and be not conformed to this world: but be ye transformed by the renewing of your mind, that ye may prove what is that good, and acceptable, and perfect will of God." (KJV)*

This states that the way we think and what we believe transforms us. Every action is rooted in a thought that produced it. What that means is that you will live out the life you believe to be a part of. You can believe to still be in Adam or you can believe you live in Christ. Adam thinks one way and Christ Jesus thinks another way.

Think death or life and peace. Let me explain a few things. It says in 2 Corinthians 10:5, *Casting down imaginations, and every high thing that exalts itself against the knowledge of God, and bringing into captivity every thought to the obedience of Christ.*

Your life has to line up with who Christ is for you. Not just your life but also how you think and what you know about who God is for you. Now, you have another way of thinking in the Spirit and your life will follow your thought life.

The problem with most of us is that we don't do this. I'm going to show you how to start training yourself. You can wear down the enemy when you get this. We will focus on what we have in Christ already. You know we already possess the mind of Christ.

> *For who hath known the mind of the Lord, that he may instruct him? But we have the mind of Christ. 1 Corinthians 2:16 (KJV).*

Remember you have a carnal mind and a Spiritual mind as well.

The key to renewed thinking is to not use the carnal mind when dealing with your identity in Christ. Understand that I am talking about logic and rational thinking so we can maneuver around in the world and deal with everyday life. We use it while in this world but it should not take the lead in our lives. We are led from the throne of God instead of getting it from the world. The world cannot teach us anything concerning the Kingdom of God. We are not from this world but God gave us our carnal mind in order to function in this world around us. Jesus did it, so we can too.

When we hear and apply this massively important message our mind will become renewed and will be functioning from the mind of Christ Jesus.

Mature Sons

The five senses of the flesh are the gateway or, in other words, the doorway the enemy uses to get into your head. So, the question is how can we stop it? I'm glad you asked! I'm going to teach you four practical ways and places to take your thoughts captive. The key to this is practice.

The Bible in Hebrews 5:12-14 talks about milk and meat; maturity and immaturity. So, the question here is how can you tell what is immature and mature? Before I get into this, I want you to know that milk isn't a bad place; it's a place of discovering. Every believer in this world has some areas where they live on milk and still need the bottle. Some believers are into meat but think they are on milk. Let me break this down for you.

Milk is a place of discovering what you don't fully know or understand. It is likened to a baby. When you have a baby, you have to teach him. At first you are super patient and understanding that he is in a season of growing. At the beginning, you will find yourself always doing things for your baby, feeding him, clothing him, changing diapers and so on. The same applies to new believers or even people who have walked with God for a while but may have not discovered Him fully. All of us will grow through these stages in our personal walk with the Father. A believer may have walked with God for 20 years and may still be living on milk in some areas. Why? Because many have a limited belief system rooted in religious works. So, it takes time for them to learn how to put off wrong thinking and to put on Jesus' new creation mindset.

So, who are meat eaters? They are the ones that have their senses exercised and trained to discern between God and the enemy. They know what is of Holy Spirit and what is of the spirit of the first Adam (natural man). Now I should mention this, scripture doesn't say you must have everything perfect to be mature. It says by use and exercise, which means the difference between milk drinkers and meat eaters, are simply using and exercising what they know. When we practice what we know, we live from maturity, we learn what is good and of God and what is evil and of Satan.

So, I encourage you in your growth to expose Satan's playbook of lies, schemes, tactics, and tricks, then get to know personally the God you serve. Not just knowing but putting into action what you know every day. It is a continual process. The key is knowing that we are okay in Christ and that we are growing into His Spiritual realities. It is amazing how patient Jesus is with us and that Holy Spirit is there to help us along the way.

Now that I have shown you the enemy's tricks and how he uses the flesh as a doorway to get into your mind, I want to give you some practical tips on how to take your thoughts captive. We have learned that the five senses are the path through which the enemy attacks sons of God.

There are four voices that will speak to you:

1. Feelings have a voice and they speak through the bodies five senses.
2. Emotions have a voice that creates a will that sounds like logic and rationale in your mind.
3. Carnality has a voice that sounds like the wisdom of a worldly, fleshly, sensual system. James 3:13-17 defines carnal wisdom as demonic. It is also the voice that brings enmity in your mind between what is true and the truth.
4. The voice of the Holy Spirit sounds like the fruit and gifts of the Spirit. Therefore, it's important to study God's word. Not just read but even listen to audios of it to train your ears to hear God's word when He speaks. Spend two plus hours a day to learn to master His voice through His word.

The key point I want to make is that knowing God's word is amazing. Knowing it through use and exercise as a lifestyle will allow you to know Him more personally.

Note that numbers 1-3 of the voices are from one person. In John 10 Jesus calls this the stranger's voice. And then number four is the voice of the Spirit of God.

Here are four areas where we might be hearing the stranger's, Satan's, voice:

1. Feelings that are controlled by carnal thoughts.
2. Emotions that are controlled by carnality.
3. Logic and rationale that is controlled by carnal thinking.
4. The will of natural man that's outside of God's will.

It is important to know that feelings, emotions, logic and the will are not bad when they are governed by the Holy Spirit. It is when carnality is controlling them that they get distorted into the demonic worldly wisdom of the spirit of the first Adam (natural man).

The greatest lesson I have learned is to ask the Holy Spirit what He thinks. When I'm in a situation, I take the thought I have and simply say "Holy Spirit what is it that you're feeling about this situation?" or "What do you think about my logical thoughts?" When we do this, taking our thoughts captive to the obedience of the Spirit of Christ, we will not carry out our fleshly will but instead carry out the will of the Father.

Mature sons govern their natural man bringing him under the obedience of their spirit man. They are quick to recognize the voice of their heavenly Father and the voice of the enemy scheming to derail them from their spirit life. As we train our thinking then we will rise up to live in the fullness of all that Christ Jesus has won for us.

CHAPTER FIVE

ALL THINGS ARE POSSIBLE

Knowledge + Application = Lifestyle Results

The Spirit's thoughts are limitless, without restriction of any kind, including toward mankind. But, the mind controlled by the flesh or ego thinks within the box of limitations. But the Spirit of the Father sees things outside the box of time, space or soul.

Do a word Bible search on the phrase 'all things' and you will be surprised how many times it appears in the scriptures. The Spirit is in "all things" and He told us that "all things" are possible for us as sons of God as well.

> *"Jesus said to him, 'If you can believe, all things are possible to him who believes.'" Mark 9:23.*

Do you still have the same faith that you had when you were born again? I asked this question because the same faith that saves you is the same faith that heals the sick and makes the impossible become possible if you believe.

Jesus also said: *"And all things you ask in prayer, believing, you will receive."* Matthew 21:22.

Believing is so uncomplicated. It is simply trusting and letting the Spirit do what He does best in us, through the divine nature in our life. We tend to miss the ease of believing because of its simplicity.

The Spirit tells us in Scripture, that when we don't know what to pray, He intercedes for us.

> *Now likewise also, the Spirit joins to help us in weakness; for we do not know the things which we should pray for as it behooves, but the Spirit Himself makes intercession with inexpressible groaning. And the one searching hearts knows*

what is the mindset of the Spirit, because He intercedes for the saints according to God." Romans 8:26-27.

Think about this, He knows we are learning, growing, and discovering who we are in Him. The same goes with believing. He knows we are learning and that He is our strength while we are discovering the assisting force within us.

Who is weak in the above verses? Only our soulish flesh is weak. So, from time to time when we act fleshly and feel weak, the Spirit understands that we are growing therefore, He helps us.

This should give us confidence that the Holy Spirit will never leave us hanging while we are growing, especially when we need Him the most. I think sometimes we complicate things or we make our identity seem like a burden. The Father is for us. He is radically crazy about us and wants us to know Him fully.

Here is a point to remember: The same belief that it took for you to believe that Jesus saved you at your salvation experience is the same belief it takes for us to believe for any area or need in our life. Jesus expanded on this concept in John 14-17. He repeated it several times in different ways, as if to a large group of slow learners. God does not think in impossibilities, only *in-all-things* kind of possibilities.

And we are to renew our mind to think like the Spirit. In fact, the only restriction of any kind placed on New Testament believers is the law of love. When all is said and done, this should be our motive, to renew our mind in love.

Think like the Spirit; all things, all possibilities, all of the time!

This formula when applied to our lives will set us up for a lifestyle of victory: *Knowledge + Application = Lifestyle Results*

When we come to the knowledge of who we are in Christ Jesus and we apply this reality then we have a lifestyle that will reflect it. It's so important to know our identity as spirit sons of God.

The Spirit of God knows who He is. You don't have to convince

Jesus that He is a Son of God. In oneness, they think from a place of complete power and authority. The Godhead knows who they are, which is how they move forward in complete power and authority.

Satan knows who the Godhead is as well, and he knows who you are abiding in, and as God's son, he knows that he is completely defeated.

Good News! The Holy Spirit, Jesus, and the Father also know who we are in them.

> *And the evil spirit answered and said to them, 'I recognize Jesus, and I know about Paul, but who are you?' Acts 19:15.*

When the enemy sees you, he sees the Father who made you in His likeness and image. How is that possible? It is possible because the same Spirit that is in Christ Jesus is in you. The Spirit of the Father and His nature is also in you. The soulish part of you is the only one that remains clueless as to who you are.

Why is that so? It is because we look from the eyes of the flesh ruled soul instead of from the Spirit, the way the Father sees us.

The Trinity knows that we are in Christ Jesus, one in Spirit, an equal rights shareholder with the Sons inheritance, strengthened with all power in our spirit. They know that we have authority over all the power of the enemy. But, as long as the sons of God do not understand this, we are powerless and are no threat to the enemy!

Again why? Because, we don't believe we have power in the likeness and image of the Spirit of God.

The Spirit of God thinks power. Hebrews 1:3 says, *He (Jesus) is the radiance of the glory of God and the exact imprint of His nature, and He upholds the universe by the word of His power. After making purification for sins, He sat down at the right hand of the Majesty on high.* (ESV). Jesus upholds all things by the word of His power! Note what it says, by His power. Jesus knew God had given Him power as His Son.

Who does Jesus say the word of God is?

> *"For the words that You have given Me I have given them,*
> *and they received them, and knew truly that I came forth*
> *from You; and they believed that You sent Me." John 17:8.*

Let us break this down; the Spirit of the Father God is the Word, according to Jesus. He is saying He can uphold all things by the Word of God, the Father, and His power. The Word of the Father is power! The Father gave all power to the Spirit of Jesus. And remember He is in us and we are in Him; as one, just like Jesus and the Father.

Jesus was the Word, and the Word was with God and the Word was God Himself. (John 1:1). Is the Father the Word? Yes!

> *"I have revealed Your name to those You have given Me*
> *out of the world. They were Yours; You gave them to Me,*
> *and they have kept Your word." John 17:6.*

Even as Jesus is the Word of God, so are we. We are the living Word of God, proclaiming our Father in heaven just like Jesus.

> *"In this, love has been perfected with us, so that we may*
> *have confidence in the Day of Judgment that, just as He is,*
> *also are we in this world." 1 John 4:17.*

I am not saying that we are Jesus, but what I am saying is that *as He is, so are we in this world.*

> *"You are from God, little children, and have overcome them*
> *[evil spirits, v. 1-3]; because greater is He Who is in us*
> *than he who is in the world." 1 John 4:4.*

Spirit sons, who know their inheritance in God, think power, authority and they think like God thinks! This becomes a lifestyle for the sons of God so they can establish the kingdom of heaven upon earth.

The Favor Plan

The Spirit of God's will for us is favor. Favor is part of the Father's nature, that is in us - so that means favor is in us. Noah found favor with God, so did Joseph, Abraham, David and Solomon.

Favor is obviously His will for His people. David said it wonderfully:

> *"For it is You who blesses the righteous man, O Lord, you surround him with favor as with a shield." Psalm 5:12.*

We can tell from their lives that favor from God was a good thing. Every blessing, including favor, is with us as Spirit sons in power.

God obviously believes that His own should have favor, with Himself and with others.

CHAPTER SIX

FINAL THOUGHTS

Our Inheritance

What I want to do in this chapter is lay a foundation on how to train our logical minds and sensual parts to live from the glory of God and the Holy of Holies every day of our lives. Each person is coming from a different perspective of life in their Christian walk. As we go through this, we will meet each of you where you are in your walk with Christ so that you can see, learn and understand.

People were separated from the life of God through the first Adam. This is because he chose the knowledge of good and evil, becoming judge of right and wrong, as opposed to the tree of life which is innocence.

Innocence can be likened to a child who makes a mistake without understanding what they are doing but remains loved. Why is that so? It is because the child hasn't learned what is good or evil. The child is just innocent, they haven't done anything wrong. So, if the child doesn't know the rule or law, then there is no transgression. Because of the child's innocence, there is no condemnation. A child can laugh, play and break the most expensive thing in your house and still run to you for love because they haven't learned to feel guilty over what's right and wrong.

Christ has given you innocence at your born-again experience. He has returned us to a place of innocence because we are under the Spirit and not the law. See, where there is no law there is no transgression, no condemnation, you are 100% innocent. So, wherever you are in your growth, you can always expect the loving nurturing Spirit of God. Why? You are innocent; Christ has removed your sinful nature.

Now, if my teenage son was to come to my house and act up breaking things, he is not innocent. This is because he has the knowledge of good and evil. He knows what is right and what is wrong. This is what happened to the first Adam after he went from not knowing good or evil, to knowing it and now faces condemnation. Adam, in his own mind, became an enemy of God.

Jesus did not come to fix us because the old man cannot be repaired, he can only be replaced. (Colossians 1:21,22). Jesus didn't come to make us a better person, He came to replace us with Himself. When someone becomes a Christian, they receive the Person of Jesus Christ, not just a free ticket to heaven. We didn't just obtain righteousness and holiness, but we received Jesus Christ and His nature. It is important to understand that Righteousness, Holiness, Truth and Faith are a person - it's the person of Jesus Christ. So, when we received the Person of Jesus, we received every bit of *who* He is. We became like Him as if we were identical twins. So, my question to you is, how righteous and holy is Christ? Jesus is one hundred percent holy and righteous. So then how holy are you? Completely holy!

This is our inheritance and it has been given to every one of us. Do you realize that all your hard work, miracles, signs and wonders, all your perfect church attendance, prayers and fasting cannot make you holy? It's only Christ who can give this to you. When you become born again you possess the very DNA of God! We have two choices to make: accept what God says and live in the innocence of His goodness or live under the wrath of the law of works. This is what religion demands. It tells us we need rules and regulations to bring balance to our lives and we must work our way into right standing with the Father. In other words, it's something to be earned by doing instead of being.

Dualistic thinking is based on the knowledge of good and evil. If I do good I get good, if I do bad I get bad, if I don't sin, if I hate the world, if I pray harder, if I go to church or if I give 10% of my income I will get closer to God.

Think this through, with this mentality are we accepting the salvation, inheritance and victory that Jesus gave us? Not really because we think we have to do certain things to make ourselves righteous. In other words, a self-made righteousness is what we get. (Romans 10:3-4). This kind of mindset is rooted in the natural man's perspective and in the knowledge of good and evil. We become the judge and create our own outcome by producing a man-made religion and gospel with the help of Satan. The knowledge of good and evil is rooted in the law and it stirs up sin and brings forth death. (Romans 4:15).

Jesus put us in His heart, raised us up and seated us in the Father, far above all principalities and powers. So, you have the righteousness of Christ. Is Christ sinning? No. Is the second Adam going to fall from grace? No. So, neither are you. Why? Because you are seated in Him on His throne. You don't have your own throne but you are an equal right shareholder in the throne of Jesus. You are one with Him. (Ephesians 2:5-6) If any man be in Christ, he is one with the Spirit of God. (1 Corinthians 6:17) You belong to Him. (1 Corinthians 6:19-20).

Most intercession and the cultures of revival are rooted here on earth. Most often we plead for God to send miracles or revivals that are only works of the flesh that stir up the realities of the dead old perspective. What happens is that we end up asking for what we think we don't have. In reality, we already have all things in Christ. People then tend to get angry or discouraged with God because they are not seeing it manifest. They are allowing their natural senses to govern them. We fall into this trap when we feel we have done all the right things but end up with nothing changed. We must understand that this belief system produces only dead results.

The knowledge of good and evil is a horrible formula for producing biblical truths not rooted in the Spirit. Rather, it contributes to a dualistic mind of good and evil. Let me give you an example of what I'm talking about. If someone has a need and they decide to fast for two weeks to obtain a certain breakthrough. But without realizing it they fast according to a fleshly formula to move God's hand in favor towards them. And then, when they give testimony of how well they fasted they unknowingly stepped into a prideful boasting of self. Pride rose up because it was accomplished through their own strength through a fleshly formula. Unknowingly, at times we fast from this dualistic mindset by taking the spiritual concept of fasting yet applying it from the strength of our flesh. There is a powerful spiritual principle in fasting when not done in the flesh.

Even when we cry, "Don't shut the heavens!" that is the mindset of knowing good and evil. If we fully understand that we are now living in heavenly places then the heavens should be available to us. But, we end up functioning from a dualistic mindset of the truth, we are in heaven – but we are locked out of it. How can our prayers be effective with the mindset that is always crying out for something that is already ours?

Here is something to think about. Many in the church today are being pastored out of the very thing that got Adam kicked out of the garden. You are either a saint or you aren't, there is no gray area. Either you are in heaven receiving all God's blessings or you're missing out on them. This is where you need to make a choice. People asked Jesus, "What must we do?" But, Jesus answered and said, "Just believe in the One who sent Me." The question is do you believe in the One Who sent Jesus? If you say yes then the work is done, you are positioned at rest in Him. The Bible tells us to strive to enter the *rest* that comes through believing. Our mind struggles to believe this. The Gospel is for everyone, it works anywhere in the world, and doesn't matter what language, education level or abilities. The Gospel is simple enough for anyone to live it out. We merely have to believe.

Most of us have been Christians our whole life and still haven't really grasped all that Jesus has done for us. I am hoping to break this down for you so that you can begin this journey of discovering all that you are in Christ.

I want you to understand the reality that the love of God is from the tree of life instead of from the tree of the knowledge of good and evil. What does this mean? God desires family and the Son wants a bride. The Gospel is all about bringing the family back together for the Father and a prepared bride for the Bridegroom. The Father has chosen you but Christ will not be unevenly yoked. He is returning for a perfect and spotless bride; not a prideful bride. He's coming for a bride like Him, who is a conqueror and ruler, and who is full of His joy.

God implemented His perfect plan and He called it the Gospel. He did this because of His love for every human being. No one comes to the Son unless the Father draws him. That means He drew you to Him. Why? It's because He is head over heels in love with you. The Father is good and He desires that you taste and see His goodness. What He started in you He will finish because you are complete in Christ.

What is amazing about this revelation of Jesus is that God is not trying to make you a better person. If you were crucified with Christ Jesus then He has replaced you with Himself. This is why the Apostle Paul says in Galatians 2:20, "It is no longer I who live". In other words, your sin nature isn't alive anymore but you now have the Spirit nature of the Father. The verse goes on to say, "the life I live I live by the faith of the Son of God." You now live through the faith of the Son and not from your own faith. Now, you identify with the faith of the Son, Jesus. Why is this so? It's because it is a gift and no one can boast outside of Christ. (Ephesians 2:8).

The Gospel is that Jesus knew us, came to us, died for us, loved us, and saved us. It isn't about what we do but about what He has already done. Everything else is simply just a response to the Gospel. The Gospel isn't about instruction; it is about the complete goodness of God. He did it all for us and finished it completely. Amazingly, as He is, so are we in this earth. (1 John 4:17) When John was writing this, he saw Jesus as He is today. He is making the statement that Jesus is now in power, authority, at rest, and seated in heavenly places. John is saying this is also who we are right now on this earth.

1 John 5:18 says, If anyone is born of God, Jesus Christ will keep him and the devil can't touch him. Most people base their Christianity upon experience, history and what they've been taught about the Bible. But the Bible really says that you are born of God, you're free from sin and the devil touches you not. The Devil isn't even relevant in your life and is God's enemy whom He has overcome. It's done. The mystery of the good news is that when you accepted Christ you

died with Him. This mystery must become real to us and to understand that we were co-crucified with Christ and rose with Him. He is the Hope of glory and He is within us. (Colossians 1:27).

You might be asking yourself how this can be. It's because we were born again in the like manner that Jesus was born.

God send His Word, Jesus, with Holy Spirit present also. When God sent His Word Mary became pregnant by the power of Holy Spirit. This is where heaven and earth came together. The Word (fully God) and Mary (fully human) brought forth God in the flesh which made Jesus fully man. This is a portrait of God's original plan that heaven and earth be united together. Christ Jesus came to give access to both the natural realities and spiritual realms once again. He was the first born of a new species, a new creation never seen before. When you receive Christ, His Spirit comes from above and is conceived in your flesh and becomes one with you. And you were born again from above making you a new creation just like Jesus as Spirit sons of God. You are new, the old has been killed and taken over by the new species and you have become just like Christ in Spirit as He is.

Under Adam is a human birth line born of the flesh (the sin nature) that died when you accepted Christ. You are now born into a new blood line and as a spiritual being from heaven above. You are not a first Adam anymore.

If any man be in Christ, He is of one Spirit with the Lord. So, you have a Spirit and it is Christ's Spirit. You are a Spirit being. This is the core of your identity, a being born from Heaven. So, we ask when was Jesus slain? He was slain before the foundation of the earth, before you were even created. (Revelation 13:8). When you accepted Christ, you received all of the inheritance that was in place before God said, "let there be light" and created the world. This means you were found in Christ before you were ever lost in Adam. You have come into a Spirit marriage and the two have become one. You have become united as one with your creator.

Now let me ask you a question. Has the Spirit of Christ ever sinned? No. Then your spirit has become that same Spirit. I'm teaching you to see from the Spirit of God's perspective. In the Spirit, we have to be able to renew our mind and train our senses in God's reality. The sins of the world have been taken away, they're gone. You live from eternity. We are not to live towards eternity, trying to reach eternity one day, but we are to live from it because we are in Christ. This is where you are right now; you have literally died and gone to heaven now. This earth body may or may not stop working, but if it does stop you don't die. Why? It's because you are a spirit who has a soul and a body. This is critical to know. You are not a soul and body; you are a Spirit being who has a soul and body. See, there is no difference between you and Jesus; you are identical twins in the Spirit of Christ. This is why Paul says, "I want to build you to the fullness of the stature of Christ."

What I want to point out first is that we have died to the old nature. Second, is that the sin nature has been finished, it has been done away with, and it has no authority or power over you whatsoever. See, the life we live we live unto God in unbroken fellowship with Him. We need to see ourselves as dead to sin, we no longer have any relations with it. Your time to sin is cut off. You now have an unbroken relationship with Christ, just like the Father and the Son, Jesus, have an unbroken fellowship. You have the same inherited unbroken relationship. (Romans 6:1-11).

Your behavior did not give you the right to receive this free gift nor can your behavior take it from you. Your attitude, understanding and lifestyle did not qualify you for this free gift. Jesus qualified you. That means your lifestyle, understanding and attitude cannot disqualify you. Nothing you do disqualifies or qualifies you for the free gift Jesus gave you. You are a new creation and you cannot be uncreated from this value. You are everything Jesus is and you are nothing He is not. What God has put together let no man separate. (Matthew 19:6). Understanding that you are one Spirit with Christ gives you the ability to treat yourself from your created value in Jesus. Is Jesus condemning himself? No, and neither should you. You are in heaven in the midst of God and angels. This is who you are and where you are from right now.

We can't treat ourselves any different than Jesus would treat Himself.

When God looks at you He sees you as the Spirit of Christ. There is no separating you and Jesus. You are now defined as Jesus defines Himself. Jesus said, "If you have seen Me, you have seen the Father." (John 14:9) So also, we need to understand that Jesus cannot see Himself outside of His Father. Why would we think it is different for us? Philippians 2:5 says, "Let this mind be in you that was also in Christ." Look at this carefully, the Bible is telling you to do something. It is saying to think the way Jesus thinks. So how does Jesus think? Verse 6 in Philippians 2 says, "He did not see it as robbery to be in equality with God." What? No. That can't be true! But the Bible said it is true. Yes, I understand the point is to be humble like Christ, but we can't skip over this vital key that we are to have the mind Jesus had concerning equality with the Spirit of God.

Every Christian asks this question, what does God require of us and what do we need to do? Jesus says that God only requires us to simply believe in the One whom He sent. So, my question is, do you believe in the One whom God sent? If you do, then all the work you have to do is done. He who entered into Christ's rest has ceased from striving. (Hebrews 4:9-11).

You are not human any more. What do I mean? You are not governed by human realities. You are in God's Spirit genre now. You are not trying to be sons of God because you are already sons. Adam was made in the image of God and when Adam opened his eyes he saw a mirror image of God and himself. Before the fall, Adam had the capacity to contain the likeness and image of God and had righteousness in God.

Colossians 2:11 says that we have been circumcised by Christ where He stripped off the whole corrupt sinful nature. The old nature in the flesh has been stripped from you and now you are a bondservant to righteousness. You want to do what you have been created for, as a spirit being, to do what the Spirit is wanting which is to bring the Spiritual realities of God to earth. The core of each one of us really just wants what God wants. God brought life through Christ so all your transgressions, past, present and even the ones that you will commit tomorrow are already forgiven. Those wrongdoings will never, ever, count against you again. (2 Corinthians 5:19). You can live guilt free, separation free, condemnation free. Anything that has guilt, shame, separation and condemnation, is removed from your life and allows you to live from God's reality.

The only thing that will separate you from Jesus is a vain imagination because every standard that has been put up against us has been brought down by Christ. Now you can never disappoint God and the devil can never touch you. This is because you have done nothing wrong since you live in the full acceptance of God. He is not counting believers' sins against them. Jesus didn't come to condemn the world. (John 3:17). He came to awaken it to the Father's reality. This is where you need to make a decision that you will never punish yourself again. Your conscience is clean and you don't have any sin on your record; this is a complete surrender to God's radical love and forgiveness to you.

God said to Abraham, take your son, your only son, the son you love to Mount Moriah and sacrifice him. Now I know there is a lot of stuff we can get out of this but let me use this one point; take your only son. Abraham had another son, Ishmael, who was probably in his thirties at this time. But, God only instructed Abraham to take Isaac to Mount Moriah. (Genesis 22) Now, why would God call Isaac Abraham's only son? It is because God wasn't going by his earthly sons. He had a spiritual perspective towards Abraham's sons. God still continues to not see anyone after the flesh. So, through God's only Son, your old nature, the flesh, does not exist. Now, you have taken on the flesh of Jesus and have obtained righteousness.

If you say you are not clean, then that gives the thought that Jesus didn't do His job on the cross. Should we rethink what we are saying about ourselves? There is only one time the Scripture says come and let's reason together. (Isaiah 1:18) Reason takes place in our minds. We have to think out, process through thought, the finished work of the cross for it to become real to us. This is the progression of renewing the mind.

Walking the Life

When the devil crucified Jesus on the cross he didn't know that you would be free from Adam's sin and would become one with Jesus. If he had known that, he wouldn't have killed Jesus. This is why it was a mystery that could only be reveled through the finished work of the cross. Satan didn't know that you would become a brand-new creation and in the same class with Christ Jesus. He now knows you are one with him and that he can't touch you because you have overcome him through Christ Jesus.

The only person you can relate to in the Gospel is Jesus. This is because He is the only person in the Gospel with the new creation of God that is born from above. You can only relate to Jesus who walked in the Spirit and was born of the Spirit of God. Every person before the cross, were un-regenerated and not saved. Yes, there were believers but no one was saved until Jesus died on the cross. You can't fully relate with those before the cross because they were under the curse of the law and you are born again and regenerated in Christ as a son.

Just as Jesus forgave everyone so we too should follow suit as ones who have been forgiven. Jesus was healing those that came to Him and He cast out demons with a word so are we to do these things because we are in Christ Jesus.

Some years ago, people believed one had to go through forgiveness and repentance before they could receive from Him. Now we know that God will touch whoever comes to Him, no matter what they've done wrong, and they will be healed. Why? It's because people have been preaching that anyone can be healed so now people expect to get healed. By hearing this truth then the faith for healing comes. Now we are teaching believe in your heart, confess with your mouth and bam it happens! It can happen this suddenly because the Greek word for salvation, *sozo*, means *saved*, *healed* and *delivered*. In other words through salvation you can't get any more delivered or healed than you already are.

The key is that we have to train our senses and mind to what has already happened in the Spirit so our soul and body will be aligned to the Spirit of God's reality. Just know that in hearing this word of faith it will happen - let it be done according to your faith. Sozo means your spirit is saved, your soul is delivered, and your body is healed. Everything that the fall of man took from us is now returned to us in Christ Jesus.

Desire is important to God and He moves from your desire. So, then what is it that you desire? Tell Him those desires. Say to God: "I want to walk out the fullness of the finished work of the cross, to have my mind and senses built up to the fullness of the stature of who I am in Christ Jesus." Jeremiah 31:34 says that God will remember your sins no more and under the New Covenant that every man will know God for themselves and no one will need to teach them. (Hebrews 8:12) The Bible says the anointing in you teaches you. The only job of the five-fold ministry is to raise you up into a mature son, from a child to an adult and from milk to meat.

True maturity knows there is no condemnation for those who are in Christ Jesus. (Romans 8:1) If God said it then it's settled. If God says you are righteous it doesn't matter what anyone else says because it was settled before the foundations of the earth. Before the white throne of judgment, you are ok, you are forgiven, and you are clean. God desires that you walk in the fullness of the stature in Christ by believing with your heart and confessing with your mouth in agreement with what the Father is speaking and doing. All we have to do is believe like a child. It seems offensive to us because we can't believe it could be that easy. See, we think understanding is believing but understanding isn't believing. Believing brings instant action. It isn't about the action of understanding, it's believing in the action of being who you are. The act of believing is simply just being. You have the joy of God, you have the faith of God, and you have the love of God.

All of this is a complete gift to you from God, a complete rescue package. Christ is here in the flesh and anything else is anti-Christ. We are seated in heavenly places, not of this world. Jesus is seated way above the seen and unseen realities and we are seated in him. So that means we are up there looking down on earth with the authority of heaven. We are to pray from heaven. Too often we pray towards heaven instead of from heaven. If we are kings of the king of kings then aren't our decrees as sons of God? We are everything that He is.

Jesus is the High Priest and King, and He has made us priests and kings too. Jesus is a first born of many brethren, a Son, so we are also His first-born son. God is always number one. He was here before us so he is first and outside that He has grafted you as His number one just like Him. His desire is to create a family. Jesus desires to be evenly yoked as the same creature as he is in the Spirit. The provision of everything Christ has done is finished and dwelling inside you. The only problem we have is that we don't know the reality that Christ and we are one.

Suppose if Jesus had your job and your boss was not promoting Him, do you think that He would fret and worry about it? No. The difference between how we would react and how Jesus would react is that we have a vain imagination. Somehow, we have allowed this to separate us from Christ. What God put together let no man separate in any way, word, deed or intention. Have you been wronged? Ask yourself if Jesus was wronged how would He deal with it? Then that is how we should deal with it. Do what Jesus does, live as He lives, and even not limited by the Jesus we see in the Gospels but living as Jesus who is seated in heaven right now. It is amazing how powerful confessing with our mouth and believing in our heart is. The only thing is for us to believe. The Spirit has all the answers and it is our soul that is aligning to the realities of the Spirit.

We are positioned to have complete victory in all areas of our life. It's ours when we *Think and Grow Christ-Minded*. It is possible to live with the mind of Christ, to walk in the fullness of Holy Spirit, seeing and doing only what the Father is doing. We can do all that Jesus did while as a man upon the earth - healing the sick, raising the dead, turning the water into wine, walking on water and multiplying the fish and loaves. This can be your reality as you align yourself with your rightful inheritance as a son of God.

In section one we have been challenged to *Think and Grow Christ-Minded.* In the following section we will discover how to apply this new mindset into a *Sonship Lifestyle* as we minister to others through everyday living.

SECTION TWO

Sonship Lifestyle:
A Mission-Minded Lifestyle Manual

CHAPTER ONE

LAYING KINGDOM FOUNDATION

To understand the Kingdom, one must first be born again of the Spirit.

> *After dark one evening, he (Nicodemus) came to speak with Jesus. 'Rabbi,' he said, 'we all know that God has sent you to teach us. Your miraculous signs are evidence that God is with you.' Jesus replied, 'I tell you the truth, unless you are born again of the Spirit, you cannot see the Kingdom of God.'* John 3:2-3.

Until you have a born again experience you will not see or comprehend the things of the Kingdom. Matthew 6:33, says, *"…seek first the Kingdom of God and His righteousness, and all these things shall be added to you"*. Seeing and comprehending the Kingdom of God should be our first priority.

Jesus said seek first the Kingdom of God and His righteousness so this is where we must begin our journey. Righteousness is our inheritance and our identity in the likeness of the Spirit of the Father and His Kingdom. God's Kingdom is where He rules and reigns in heaven and earth. God knows that when we have His Kingdom then we have all that is His.

The Kingdom of God Has to Become Your Reality

What does that look like? A key word I want to begin with is "see." Jesus told Nicodemus that at a person's born again experience they begin to "see." Meaning their eyes are opened so they can see into the Kingdom realm like the Father, Son and Holy Spirit. In John 3:6, Jesus tells Nicodemus that the Spirit, which is the realm of the Kingdom, is like the wind, it comes and goes. And though we can't see it, we see the effects of the Kingdom. Without the ability to "see" we can't understand the things of the Kingdom.

It is important for us to know what the Kingdom of God is in heaven and on earth. One main key to understand is that the Kingdom is actually a Person who is the Spirit of God.

The Kingdom is to be brought to the world:

> *"And this gospel of the kingdom will be preached in all the world as a witness to all the nations, and then the end will come."* Matthew 24:14.

What is the gospel of the kingdom of God? The gospel is the good news that Jesus took away all our sins that had us separated from God and that we are now reconciled back to the Father. We are to go preach this message to all the world. But then what is the kingdom of heaven? It is God's home, residence, dwelling place. That question leads us to ask, what is the kingdom of God? Romans 14:17 says that it is righteousness, joy and peace in the Holy Spirit. It is the rule and reign of God.

God's desire was for man to have dominion on earth from the very beginning. (Genesis 1:26). First Adam lost that dominion when they fell into sin. But second Adam, Jesus, took back the lost dominion and handed it to those who are born again through God's Spirit.

So, it is also important to understand what the Kingdom of God is not. Scripture says it isn't a matter of talk or about what you eat or drink. (1Corithinthians 4:20; Romans 14:17).

The Kingdom of God is not like a natural, physical or carnal realm. It is the unseen, it is not about words but action. The Kingdom of God is moving and active.

So, where is the Kingdom of God? For unbelievers the Kingdom is near them. As a believer, the Kingdom is in you:

Now when He was asked by the Pharisees when the Kingdom of God would come He answered them and said, the Kingdom of God does not come with observation; Nor will they say, see here! Or see there! For indeed, the kingdom of God is within you. (Luke 17:20-21).

Naturally, nobody can see the kingdom unless they are born again. It is invisible to the naked eye. We must discover the kingdom of God in us. The Spirit has to become real to us, so that we can know what it is in us. Knowing this, we can begin to see and think kingdom minded.

By discovering the kingdom, it makes us:

- Settled
- Relaxed
- Confident

The kingdom is the Spirit of God in us. So, what then does that look like? We can see the fruits of the Spirit within our lives. Some of these fruits are:

- Peace
- Joy
- Boldness
- Love in the Spirit
- Healing, both physical and emotional
- People getting set free

Note: Don't get frustrated with the discovery process. We are all learning and will always be learning in some area of our lives. Just relax and keep renewing yourself to the Truth that you are lacking nothing. At the moment, you might not know what's going on, but the truth is you lack nothing in Christ Jesus and you are discovering all you have in Him. (1 Corinthians 2:12).

Don't Be Afraid to Make Mistakes.

I give you permission to make mistakes. If you are not making mistakes you probably aren't growing or learning new things and changing the world around you. It's ok to make mistakes. Good leaders make room for people to make mistakes, allowing others to grow.

One reason people don't take risks is because fear is attached to it. When we take steps by faith (taking a risk) we allow Holy Spirit to teach us how to function in a new mindset which frees us from fear.

Kingdom Thinking

Every thought or action is rooted in the thought that produced it. When the Spirit governs the soul and body, the Spirit's fruit is evident. We will produce the fruit of what rules our lives:

- Fleshly thoughts give birth to carnal sensual feelings.
- Soulish thoughts bear logic and rationalization rooted in the flesh.
- Emotions come from your thought life.
- The will of man comes from the mind and senses that governs him.

What do you think gives birth to your actions? For instance, if you think you can't make it, then you are not going to make it.

Note: Learn to ask the Spirit what His thoughts are about any situation you are facing and how to handle it. Use the answer He gives you as the base to renew your mind to always think in that pattern.

Job was thinking about his fears when he said, *"the thing I feared has come upon me."* (Job 3:25). Our thoughts can create false realities to manifest around us.

Everything about the kingdom of heaven is governed by a law, the law of love. Love is the wealth of heaven and His promises are its currency.

Note: There are two laws in play!

- The law of heaven; the unseen realm.
- The law of the natural; the visible realm.

The law of the natural is governed by the Kingdom of God. That's why there is healing for the sick and all the gifts of the Holy Spirit. And these gifts function from love, joy and peace.

Where is Jesus seated right now? Colossians 3:1-2: says, *"If then you were raised with Christ, seek those things which are above, where Christ is, sitting at the right hand of God. Set your mind on things above, not on things on the earth."* I want you to see how Jesus is there in heaven and also, here in you. There, refers to heaven, celestial and spirit. Here, refers to the earth, terrestrial and physical.

Ephesians 2: 6 says Jesus, *raised us up together, and made us sit together in the heavenly places in Christ Jesus.* Therefore, that means we are in heaven seated in Christ right now. So, we are through the Spirit there in heaven and also physically here on earth.

Scripture says we are of Spirit:

> *But you are not in the flesh (terrestrial) speaking of sin nature, but in the Spirit (celestial) The nature of God, if indeed the Spirit of God dwells in you. Now if anyone does not have the Spirit of Christ, he is not His.* Romans 8:9 (NKJV, emphasis mine).

We need to have the mindset that we are citizens of heaven, which is Spirit, and also citizens here on earth.

This explains why you can call down heaven; you literally host heaven on earth! Because of Jesus in you, you are a magnet to all of heaven because the Person of Heaven dwells in you.

Everything we do was modeled by Jesus.

> *Then Jesus answered and said to them, "Most assuredly, I say to you, the Son can do nothing of Himself, but what He sees the Father do; for whatever He does, the Son also does in like manner."* John 5:19.

Our daily thoughts must be rooted in the mind of Christ. And that's why Philippians 2:5-8 says, *"let this mind be in you which was also in Christ Jesus, who, being in the form of God, did not consider it robbery to be equal with*

God, but made Himself of no reputation, taking the form of a bond servant, and coming in the likeness of men. And being found in appearance as a man, He humbled Himself and became obedient to the point of death, even the death of the cross."

Further 1 John 2:6 says, *"He who says he abides in Him ought himself also to walk just as He walked."* We are to live and think like Jesus did. It is a good idea to get in the habit of asking Holy Spirit for His opinion on anything that you are facing. Renew your mind to match what the Spirit tells you.

Understanding Kingdom Authority

The kingdom and its authority are your positions in the Spirit. The kingdom literally flows from you and it reveals who the Father is. It affects all that is around you, everything you touch, speak, do, and even your shadow manifests the glory of God. (Psalm 121:5). Everywhere your feet step is affected by the kingdom in you. Kingdom authority is a commission given to you by God. (Luke 10:19). It's been His desire to give you this from the beginning.

Gen 1:26 says He gave Adam dominion. It has always been God's desire for you to have His inherited authority and dominion with the ability to function from His Spirit. Your sonship gives you the right to function in kingdom authority and power.

> *He came unto His own, and His own received Him not. But as many as received Him, to them gave He power to become the sons of God, even to them that believe on His name which were born, not of blood, nor of the will of the flesh, nor of the will of man, but of God.* John 1:11-13 (KJV).

We are co-heirs with Christ, we have been given the inheritance as equal right shareholders in the Spirit.

> *For ye have not received the spirit of bondage again to fear; but ye have received the Spirit of adoption, whereby we cry, Abba, Father. The Spirit itself beareth witness with our*

spirit, that we are the children of God: And if children, then heirs; heirs of God, and joint-heirs with Christ; if so be that we suffer with Him, that we may be also glorified together. Romans 8:15-17 (KJV).

We have been given His Glory. (Hebrews 2:7). You have also been given the right to be one with the Father and Jesus Christ. So, If Jesus has given you something it's vital we take ownership and run with it. (Hebrews 2:1, 3a). Why? Because you're coming into agreement with the Godhead who brings Glory to the Father. (John 17:22).

Every believer has a legitimate right to exercise power and dominion and yes that includes you! Because Jesus is seated at the right hand of the Father on the throne of power and authority, and you are seated with him. (Ephesians 1:17-21, 2:6).

Take a moment, close your eyes and imagine what this Scripture looks like: what if we really believed in what we know and what would our life look like today?

It is from this place of authority that we minister the Kingdom of God as we go about our everyday business. Even the demons recognize sons of God who walk in kingdom authority:

> *And the evil spirit answered and said, Jesus I know, and Paul I know; but who are you?* Acts 19:15.

Our Bodies are the Temple of the Holy Spirit

The Father gave us the Holy Spirit to be our teacher, helper and comforter. Scripture says Holy Spirit could not be sent to the earth until Jesus was glorified. (John 7:39). Why? Because the Father wanted Holy Spirit to see Jesus in His glorified state according to Revelation 1:12-14. So, on the day of Pentecost He was released to mold us, teach us, train us into the full wisdom, knowledge, image and likeness of Jesus. In other words, as He is now, in heaven, after the cross. (1John 4:17).

It's vital we recognize Holy Spirit and learn to live in Him. Jesus lives in us by His Spirit. I cannot express with words the importance of communicating daily and listening to the Spirit.

In the Old Testament God dwelled in a man-made structure. When we look at the tabernacle of Moses we see it consisted of a courtyard, inner court and the holy of holies. The holy of holies or the most holy place was where God's presence dwelt. Jesus ended the physical structure and made us His temple. 1 Corinthians 6:19 says, *do you not know that your body is the temple of the Holy Spirit, who is in you, whom you have received from God and you are not your own.* We now are the embodiment of God.

The Bible teaches that the nature of God is three-fold; Father, Son and Holy Spirit and that God created us in His Image. (Gen 1:27). He gave us His Spirit and put Himself in our spirit and body. I Thessalonians 5:23 says the God of peace sanctify you through and through and that our whole spirit, body and soul be kept blameless at the coming of our Lord Jesus Christ. Our spirit is the place Holy Spirit comes to dwell when we become born again believers. Through Christ Jesus the Spirit makes our body the most holy place. Holy Spirit lives intertwined with our spirit which God quickened at our born-again experience.

Our soul is our character, emotions and mind and it is through our bodies that we interact with the physical world. To help us here on earth, Jesus said He would send us a helper, counselor and a teacher who will transform us into His glorified image of today.

> *And I will pray the Father, and He will give you another Helper, that He may abide with you forever the Spirit of truth, whom the world cannot receive, because it neither sees Him nor knows Him; but you know Him, for He dwells with you and will be in you. I will not leave you orphans; I will come to you.* John 14:16-18.

Another promise Jesus gave to us is that He would not leave us as orphans.

> *But the Helper, the Holy Spirit, whom the Father will send*

in My name, He will teach you all things, and bring to your remembrance all things that I said to you. John 14:26.

However, when He, the Spirit of truth, has come, He will guide you into all truth; for He will not speak on His own authority, but whatever He hears He will speak, and He will tell you things to come. He will glorify Me, for He will take of what is Mine and declare it to you. John 16:13-14.

The Holy Spirit Empowers Us

Acts 1:8 says, *"But you shall receive power when the Holy Spirit has come upon you; and you shall be witnesses to Me in Jerusalem, and in all Judea and Samaria, and to the end of the earth."* We can all receive this same power that Holy Spirit released upon every believer. We can ask Holy Spirit for knowledge, wisdom and help in discovering His power within. As He leads us we are learning from Him. He is our friend and partner in ministry and life. As God's temple we need to expect His gifts to flow out of us who are living by the Spirit. We can expect words of knowledge, prophesy, discernment and insight to begin to be released from us. Holy Spirit is ready to speak to us just as He did to Philip when He said, "go near and overtake this chariot" in Acts 8:29.

The Holy Spirit longs to fellowship with us and for us to become aware of His presence in us. We literally become the outpouring of the supernatural power that people are praying for in healing, signs and wonders. Our continual growth in relationship with Him is vital. He will teach us, guide us and lead us into amazing adventures in God.

Learning to Focus on Jesus

There is so much in the world that we end up focusing on. Much of it is on the natural world instead of the spirit world of God. So, we need to redirect our focus onto that which is life giving.

Looking unto Jesus, the author and finisher of our faith,

who for the joy that was set before Him endured the cross, despising the shame, and has sat down at the right hand of the throne of God. Hebrews 12:2.

This is a profound scripture. I will get into detail later in our section on faith, but I want you to see how Jesus is the author and finisher of our faith. That means Jesus 'invented' faith, not us. Here's a question to think about: If Jesus is the beginning and end of faith, then is Galatians 2:20 really about our faith or is it His faith?

Note: Even when praying for the sick, our focus should be on Jesus. Don't focus on the issue you are praying for, keep your eyes on the answer, Jesus.

Peter learned that things didn't fare well for him when he took his eyes off Jesus:

> *Now in the fourth watch of the night Jesus went to them, walking on the sea. And when the disciples saw Him walking on the sea, they were troubled, saying, "It is a ghost!" And they cried out for fear. But immediately Jesus spoke to them, saying, "Be of good cheer! It is I; do not be afraid." And Peter answered Him and said, "Lord, if it is You, command me to come to You on the water." So, He said, "Come." And when Peter had come down out of the boat, he walked on the water to go to Jesus. But when he saw that the wind was boisterous, he was afraid; and beginning to sink he cried out, saying, "Lord, save me!" And immediately Jesus stretched out His hand and caught him, and said to him, "O you of little faith, why did you doubt?"* Matthew 14:25-31.

Peter was walking on water and He took his eyes off Jesus when he looked at the problem around him. He focused on the big waves and it caused him to fear and lose sight of Jesus.

The carnal mind, logic and rationalization become the author of doubt. When believers believe in a lie, it can paralyze them like doubting Thomas, who said "I will do nothing unless I see him." If we trust in the lie of the logical mind it will cause us to do nothing.

Don't panic when you're faced with things that look impossible. Just relax and do your part in letting Jesus do His will through you. When nothing seems to be happening, just know a lot more than what you see is taking place. Don't rush. Pray from the place of rest and silently ask the Spirit what He thinks of the situation. When He answers you, tell yourself that all things are possible. Begin to thank God in your situation and allow the Spirit to stir boldness and confidence in you and know that Jesus has got your back.

Just know God is always in control even if the situation seems messy. Keep your eyes on Jesus and His faith working through you. The new man doesn't lack faith, it's functioning from the carnal mind that loses faith and believes in the lie. In Christ Jesus we lack nothing.

Always remember that Jesus promised you the Comforter for those times you are feeling down.

The Mind vs. the Carnal Mind

Everything God created is good so that means our mind is good. The mind is a powerful instrument that God gave us. Through the mind we have: engineers, lawyers, doctors, NASA space programs, inventors, planes, sky scrapers, cars, houses and the list goes on. The mind gives us an amazing ability to learn, produce and create.

The carnal part of the mind fights against God. The carnal mind pertains to the flesh speaking through its passions, appetites and all that is sensual. The carnal mind is not spiritual, it is human, worldly and temporal and thinking according to natural reasoning and is governed by the sensual faculties of what it can touch, feel, see, hear, taste.

But why does the carnal mind fight against God? It's because it functions in the realm of logic and rationale. The carnal mind's desires, passions and appetites are against God's desire, passion and appetite.

There are spiritual realities that the Spirit can impact the natural senses in, like through the idea of *to taste* and *see* the goodness of God for example. (Psalm 34:8).

Our minds/brains can be renewed to think like Christ Jesus. (Philippians 2:5-9). But the carnal mind can never be renewed. The carnal mind can only think according to its master, the dead old man. (Romans 6:6-11). By putting off the carnal mind, you are agreeing that the old man is dead to you and you don't listen to his voice. Your logical mind and senses can be trained and renewed. (Romans 12:2, Hebrews 5:14).

Why does the mind need to be renewed? Before your salvation experience, the flesh and the carnal mind were teaching and training your logic and senses. When you became born-again, you were given the ability to see spiritual things and kingdom truths. (John 3:3). You also inherited a new mind, the mind of Christ. (1 Corinthians 2:16).

By renewing the mind to see things as Jesus sees them, we begin to understand how all things are possible in Christ. God functions from faith and it's rooted in His being and it isn't a natural faith. The kingdom functions in the unseen.

Therefore:

- Train your natural mind to function from the mind of Christ and the unseen kingdom instead of believing fleshly logic and rationale.
- Train your mind to trust in the finished work of the cross and function from Christ's faith.
- If the mind wants to embrace fleshly logic then train it to say no and allow the new man to tell your mind to trust and have faith in the Son of God who is within.

Renewing the mind is simply taking what you've learned in the Spirit and applying it in your everyday life. Fasting is a great tool to help us shift ourselves away from our fleshly focus and cause us to concentrate on the ways of the Spirit.

Here are some important points about fasting:

- I don't fast to get anointed or to have a breakthrough. Why? Because in Christ and the new man in me it is impossible for me to get any more anointed or have a greater breakthrough than I already have in Christ Jesus
- I fast to keep the flesh of my body and the carnal part of my realities in subjection to the Spirit. By fasting it trains the mind to learn and function from the Spirit of God.

The Bible says we should cast down every high thing and imagination that exalts itself above the knowledge of God. (2 Corinthians 10:5). When taking thoughts captive, learn to present them before Holy Spirit and ask Him what He thinks of those particular thoughts. Take Holy Spirit's answer and replace the thoughts in your mind. Renew your mind by doing what Holy Spirit tells you. Applying this is what exercises the senses and renews the mind into the perspective of God.

If your carnal mind acts up, treat it like you would a child you are disciplining! Ground your carnal realities by putting the flesh on a fast!

Key truths:

- The mind of Christ in the Spirit hosts the kingdom within us.
- We need to learn to take ownership of what is ours in Christ Jesus by not giving into our flesh.
- Jesus Christ is Grace and He has a mind that thinks like the Spirit of God who has nothing missing or broken. (Titus 2:11). Therefore, we too have nothing missing or broken because Christ is in us.
- As sons of God our inheritance is in Jesus and when we are born-again He moves into us and all He received from the Father moves into us as well.

Tell me, if God is in heaven and you are here then how do you produce the kingdom? The Bible teaches us that the kingdom is in us, so that means it has to come out of us. It comes out of our identity.

Who is our identity? It's the Spirit of Jesus.

The Bible says that Jesus intercedes for you day and night. That means He is saying something concerning you right now. What is He saying? Is He giving you compliments or complaining? What is He doing? The Bible also says that Holy Spirit is praying for us and He is continually teaching us something.

What is He saying to you right now? Take a journal and begin to ask Holy Spirit and Jesus what they are saying concerning you. Write it down and start learning to dialogue with Them and from this place prophesies will flow and you'll learn to hear Holy Spirit. Think this through: If the writers of the Bible had not journaled what the Spirit told them then we would never have had the Bible.

Understanding the New Man in You

Through Christ Jesus we have now become a completely new person.

- And that you put on the new (kainos) man which was created according to God, in true righteousness and holiness. Ephesians 4:24.
- And have put on the new (neos) man who is renewed in knowledge according to the image of Him who created him. Colossians 3:10.

This scripture paints a picture of our new identity; the newness of life. There are two major Greek words used to describe what new means in these verses:

- One word is neos which means regenerated or recent. In layman's terms it's what God is doing in you, the newest recent thing. It's something that is new and still progressing. It can also be your most recent experience.
- The Second word is kainos which means fresh, new in quality and character.

Therefore, our new identity is regenerated, fresh and new in quality which is completely different from the old man. So, this identity is new:

- In the heavenly sense
- As being Christ-like
- In being glorious
- In nature

Romans 6: 3-18 is a passage you should read once a week. This is because it is very clear about what happened to the old man and what transpires at our born-again experience.

In Christ we have been given a new life. But, even if you don't understand it fully or function in its fullness doesn't mean the new man isn't present in your life.

We are positioned in Christ Jesus:

> *If then you were raised with Christ, seek those things which are above, where Christ is, sitting at the right hand of God. Set your mind on things above, not on things on the earth.* Colossians 3:1-2.

So, if we are seated with Jesus in heaven then:

- We live above
- We think above
- We talk above
- We walk above

Here are further scripture references that talk about who you are in your new identity:

- Ephesians 1:3
- Colossians 1:3
- Philippians 3:20
- Matthew 18:18 – Your sonship gives you the right. If you ask for it, you have it. Jesus said it!

- Ephesians 2:6
- Ephesians 4:20-32

Discovering Your Identity

The first Adam began to live from the carnal mind when he fell into sin. But Jesus, the second Adam stripped off the old mind and renewed it. So, the mind of Christ says, "it is finished. I completed you. You are who the Father says you are." We need to allow our mind to be renewed to think like Jesus. Thinking from the mind of Christ allows you to live every day in the fullness of who God is in you. Thinking like Adam can only bring death but thinking like Christ brings life.

God's prophetic word is a promise to us. God said, *let Us make man in Our own image, according to Our likeness.* (Genesis 1:26). God Himself said He made you to be like Him and to have His image. Our identity comes from the Spirit of God, therefore, the key to discovering our identity is learning the Spirit's identity through our Savior Jesus Christ.

What then does God look like? What are the characteristics and nature of God? What are His attributes? I've put together a list of all that Jesus is (at least what I have in my mind because Jesus is so much more). The list shows who Jesus is and because we are in Him, the characteristics apply to us also. As you discover who you are in Him, God will become more real to you. God is more than just an emotion or a feeling or some words on a paper. The reality of who God is will sink in your mind and build you up in your most holy faith. It will go beyond your natural senses and you will understand your oneness with Christ, not just in theory but in reality. (Galatians 1:16).

But to walk in your full identity in Christ takes time. I often say that there are three phases:

> Phase One: This is the light-bulb-moment. This is the point when you first get it. The moment when you understand that you are a son of God and a new creation.

Phase Two: At this point we experience the renewing of our minds. In this process, we learn to take our thoughts to Jesus and ask Him whether He is the source or what He thinks about them. The answer He gives is what we will focus our mind on and cast down any thought that is contrary to what Jesus has said.

Phase Three: This is the phase where you become all that you have been the whole time without realizing it. At this point you achieve the potential that has been hidden in you and you begin living it out. This is also a phase of growth because Christ is in you and you will begin to discover that for yourself. Here you find you lack nothing and you begin to overcome the rational mind and senses that says you're limited. You get to see yourself as God sees you.

Note: We are so full of God it's impossible to get more of Him! But what we do is grow and get a greater understanding as well as a revelation of what is already in us through Christ. It is vital to know who God is. (Ephesians 1:16 -17).

Let's pray!

I pray for insight and understanding in your life, setting your hearts and minds on things above, so that you may begin to learn to think and function like God. That you will develop and be rooted and grounded in the kingdom mentality and heavenly perspective. I don't pray that you have more faith, I pray that you may understand that you already have the fullness of the faith of the Son of God. In Jesus name, Amen.

God never had an identity crisis!

CHAPTER TWO

MINISTRY OF RECONCILIATION & OUTREACH/EVENTS

The ministry of reconciliation is an amazing way to reach out and show the world the kingdom of God. And it is simple! It is all accomplished through friendship and relationship.

I like to call it Friendship Evangelism. It's about making a friend to express God's passionate love for them and release the kingdom of heaven to the lost and hurting. This kind of ministry allows you to connect firsthand with people wherever God has called you to. Doing it over and over again makes it a lifestyle.

There are so many aspects of market place ministry; it could be your work, business, school, family and friends, daily activity or door to door outreach. The thing is, everything in your life is a potential mission field.

The most amazing thing about a mission lifestyle is that whether you are a novice or a seasoned Christian, through this manual, you are going to be equipped for the work of ministry. You will discover a friendship-fueled mission lifestyle with no pressure to perform. You will become relaxed as you function as a son or daughter in Christ as you minister reconciliation to the world around you through acts of love, healing and prophesy.

The ministry of reconciliation is a gentle ministry that ushers in compassion, grace and mercy by simply expressing the presence and power of Holy Spirit who dwells in God's children. This ministry is about functioning from the peace that surpasses all human understanding and realities of this world in the midst of the hustle and bustle of everyday life.

As spiritual sons/daughters of God we give the world the love, joy and peace it is longing for. Through a life of friendship, you build relationships which create stepping stones for the ministry of reconciliation. This leads people to the overwhelming love of Abba Father and Christ Jesus.

Many Christians are trying to get people to commit to Jesus without them ever getting to experience Him. Think about this approach for a moment: Let's take a husband and wife for example, would they get into a relationship without knowing if the other person is someone they like or want to be with? The desire to be with someone for life comes through discovering how amazing each other are, drawing closer and then becoming a couple. They see and experience the good things about each other. It is the same with relationship with God.

Friendship evangelism allows us to let people encounter God's love, peace, power and presence. Many people don't read the Bible so they need to be shown by Christians who live out the Word through God's love. The only Jesus people will ever come to know is the Jesus we show people through our lives.

We often tell people, "God requires you to repent before you can experience His love and goodness." Strangely, that isn't what Scripture teaches. It says that it's the goodness of God that leads one to repentance. (Romans 2:4). Seeing God's goodness is what turns people away from their God-less lifestyle and causes them to desire continual relationship with Him.

Lifestyle Versus Events

What is a lifestyle? A way of life or style of living that reflects the attitudes and values of a person.

A Bible verse that best describes a ministry lifestyle is Matthew 10:7 where Jesus sends out His disciples saying: And as you go, preach, saying, 'The kingdom of heaven is at hand.

When I read this and meditate upon it, I see Jesus describing a way of life He wanted His disciples to embrace and live. For Christians today "as you go" is our going into our workplace, school, marketplace, sporting events, and functions with friends and family.

I can hear His passionate heart saying to us "go proclaim that the Kingdom of our Father is near." What's really amazing is that Jesus impacted lives through His daily lifestyle while demonstrating the reality of God's Kingdom.

After telling His disciples to get out of their comfort zone and go, He says in verse 8 of Matthew 10, *Heal the sick, cleanse the lepers, raise the dead, cast out demons. Freely you have received freely give.* Surprisingly, what Jesus directed them to do is only a portion of it because love is the exponential power behind the physical display. The visual demonstrations are simply allowing people to see the living and active kingdom of God and His radical love you are proclaiming.

It isn't all about the event of your outreach but a lifestyle of love and naturally reaching out to people that brings lasting change to lives.

Outreach Through Love

In showing God's love there isn't a need for detailed planning. Make it pressure-free as you go build relationships while you supernaturally release the kingdom. Any act of love and kindness reveals a kingdom lifestyle.

Note: There is no pressure to perform. It's all about relationships, friendships and love.

When an opportunity presents itself just be who you are as a son or daughter of God and make friends. The vital key is to just "be" you.

What does "be" mean anyway? It is interesting to know that it means:

- Equal in meaning: having the same connotation
- To identify with: to constitute the same idea or object
- To constitute as the same class as
- To have a specified qualification or characterization

- To belong to the class of its creation
- To have an objective existence

To have reality or actuality, I think, therefore I am, to have, maintain, or occupy a place, situation, or position.

Therefore, just be who you are in the Spirit. Build friendships, help others and you will see things that will blow your mind. Words of encouragement, edification, and building up others are very effective in showing love. I have seen these in action as I traveled around the world and it has touched more lives than anything else.

People aren't concerned with how much you know or what you can do until they know how much you care.

Events Outreach

Let us now look at events. What is an event? It is a planned public or social occasion.

Events are great and I love doing them. Whether I'm scheduling a mission across the world, a church outreach or training, I just love it! And I personally encourage you to plan events that God puts in your heart and use the event to reveal a lifestyle. However, one of the common things I see during events is that people feel pressured which makes them uneasy and tense.

I often tell my students to always view each opportunity God gives you not as an event or mission trip, but as a chance to build friendships and relationships while serving.

As you go to that place or event, taking on the lifestyle approach will help you relax and free yourself from the pressure to perform. The only person who feels pressure is the one who's mind and senses are in need of training by the Spirit as He quickens us through compassion.

Training Our Ego-Senses to be Submitted to the Spirit of God

When the Spirit of God is allowed to govern our spirit then it will train our flesh's five senses and our logical mind to submit to His ways. If your soul, mind, will and emotions aren't renewed it will try to convince you that it is your master. For example: the flesh will think it has a choice outside of God's will. The soul will feel uneasy and uncomfortable. Your logical mind will try to make excuses by talking you out of going past your comfort zone.

Let us first understand a simple truth so that we can know why the flesh will try to go against what the Spirit says.

> *For the flesh lusts against the Spirit, and the Spirit against the flesh; and these are contrary to one another, so that you do not do the things that you wish.* Galatians 5:17

> *But you are not in the flesh but in the Spirit, if indeed the Spirit of God dwells in you.* Romans 8:9a.

You were created in the image and likeness of the Father. Therefore, your spirit is in the likeness of the Spirit of the Father and the Son. The Spirit is the identity of God the Father and God the Son. The spirit of (put your name here) is the root of your identity in the Father and the Son.

Your untrained and unrenewed senses and mind will never feel like praying for the sick or stepping out with boldness to witness for Christ. It will make all kinds of excuses. The most used is: Evangelism is not my calling. The Scripture says it is. I agree, everyone has their own preference, some like to preach on the street corners, heal in the malls while others like to prophesy and exhort at the grocery store. All in all, everyone is called to the ministry of reconciling the lost to Christ Jesus. (Matthew 28:19-20).

No matter what form of evangelism you like best we are all called to share our faith in Christ with people. I like the friendship approach; just going out there and building new relationships daily. We all can do that and it's an easy way of creating opportunities to reach out and meet the needs of the groaning world.

The Bible teaches us that we were given by Jesus the ministry of reconciliation to the lost and to the body of Christ. (2 Corinthians 5:18). On the other hand, there is no need to make a system or formula out of this. The key is simply to be in Christ, let go of feeling like you have to perform.

You are fashioned after the likeness and image of the Father Who is molding your soul to line up with kingdom thinking, perspective, attributes and nature.

The soul and flesh are not necessarily bad. What's bad is the unrenewed mind being governed by sensual desires of the flesh that hasn't reckoned itself dead. (Romans 6:11). God made your whole being good, it just needs to align with who Jesus recreated you to be.

Let us look at these Scriptures:

> Now may the God of peace Himself sanctify you completely; and may your whole spirit, soul, and body be preserved blameless at the coming of our Lord Jesus Christ. 1 Thessalonians 5:23.

Walk in the Sprit as you go and you will not heed to the desires of the fleshly senses. Because of the Spirit of Christ within you the fruit of the Spirit will manifest and all of heaven will gravitate towards you.

The flesh fears but the Spirit is fearless. Walking in the Spirit is walking out a fearless lifestyle.

> But the fruit of the Spirit is love, joy, peace, long-suffering, kindness, goodness, faithfulness, gentleness, self-control. Against such there is no law. And those who are Christ's have crucified the flesh with its passions and desires. If we live in the Spirit, let us also walk in the Spirit. Galatians 5:22-25.

Fear is not of the Spirit of God. Those ruled by fear are controlled and governed by logic and fleshly realities instead of led by the Spirit.

The Scripture says perfect love casts out fear.

> *There is no fear in love; but perfect love casts out fear, because fear involves torment. But he who fears has not been made perfect in love.* 1 John 4:18.

The areas we fear are red flags to the places in our lives where we need to discover the love of God. (Ephesians 3:19). Love is the fruit of the Spirit. A person who is not made perfect in love is the one who is not grounded deep in the Spirit. Perfect love comes from the Spirit in you.

Remember this is a lifestyle. We are all growing and learning as we go.

The flesh/soul needs to be renewed to the Truth in the Spirit of Christ; to be governed by the Spirit's realities and not our mind with its emotional realities and belief systems. First, we need to actively be learning and growing. We ought to guard against justifying daily habits that stop us from growing. But don't get frustrated with the process.

Remember God gave us dominion to rule over carnality. We are meant to have dominion over the flesh, emotions, mind and senses. (Hebrews 5:13-14). The carnal mind is only bad when the world system, flesh and sensual desires rule over you. But when the Spirit governs your mind and body, then it's called the mind of the Spirit. When we live in the Spirit, the Spirit of God becomes our reality.

When we are doing events, we need to allow Holy Spirit to lead us instead of our flesh. Staying in God's perfect love will keep us in His perfect peace where we have ears to hear what the Spirit is saying.

Practical Tip:

When you are at an event, start by telling your soul, mind, will and emotions to relax. Tell your mind that "this isn't only an event but it is an opportunity to make friends, help people and bring them into encounters with the Spirit." It is important to know that the carnal ruled mind will come against being taught new truth and won't allow the Spirit to renew it.

Points to note:

- The Spirit is willing, the Spirit is bold, the Spirit does not fear. (Proverbs 28:1). This will help bring your flesh to a place where you don't feel pressured to perform.
- When your flesh doesn't feel like doing anything, train it to know that it is the Spirit's will to do it. (Take captive every thought).
- When your logic and senses tell you that you are not bold, tell yourself that the Spirit within me is bold. (The righteous are as bold as a lion).

Remember to always keep it simple, easy and have fun; you are making friends.

I had a team of about 25 missionaries in Las Vegas and we were all just hanging out on the streets. As we all broke off into teams, I took my group for some hands-on training. As they followed me, I knew they were thinking, "PaulyB is going to pray for someone". Instead, we walked up and down the streets twice and then I looked back and said, "Hey everyone, are you ready now?" I giggled on the inside as I looked at their expressions that said, "Duh PaulyB that's why we are with you!"

"Let's go to Starbucks and have coffee" I told them. I knew they were probably wondering if they had come all the way just to sit around. But I had a plan! It was to teach them to have fun, relax and enjoy what Vegas had to offer.

As we were enjoying our beverages, we started talking to a man sitting next to us. As we listened to him share about himself he soon opened up and told us about his back injury. After a while, we asked him on a scale of 1-10, 10 being the worst, what the level of his pain was? He said, "like a 12". Then I said, "Sir, can I show you something?" He said sure. So, I took his hand in mine and we prayed for the healing of his back. God touched him with His love and his pain decreased. We finished ministering by blessing he and his wife for we knew Holy Spirit would continue what He had started in his life.

Over the next hour we met five other amazing people. We saw four out of five people experience an instant manifestation of healing in their bodies. During this time, we even bought people coffee while we had a great time fellowshipping together.

Let me say, this is not a numbers game. It is not about how many people are healed or saved. It's not even about the event of going out to minister but it's about reconciliation and bringing people into a love encounter with the living God. Even if you only reach one person or you reach a hundred it must always be about God's love not numbers.

Key Tip:

- Just relax
- Make friends
- Do something for someone
- It is only the senses and logical mind that doesn't want to "go"

I wanted to show my team a relationship-based ministry lifestyle. To show them a way of reaching out to the world without pressure; giving them the freedom to enjoy their surrounding and just "be" who God created them to be in the Spirit.

Many people have different ways of doing evangelism, but I wanted these missionaries, and you reading this book, to see something that could be incorporated into everyday activities without pressure. This is something we can all do while having fun, shopping, working or doing business while we present the kingdom of God and touch lives. Everywhere we go, we can release the life within us.

CHAPTER THREE

HEALING IN MINISTRY

Faith

Faith sees what appears impossible as a mere momentary obstacle to overcome. The impossible actually declares what faith has already done in Jesus!

The scripture says Jesus is the Author and Finisher of our faith. Jesus gave every man a portion of faith whether a believer or non-believer. (Romans 12:3).

There are two types of faith. One kind of faith is the one based on what you can touch feel, hear, taste and see. The kind of faith that makes you know that a chair will hold you up when you sit on it. This kind of faith is scientifically proven. This faith makes you believe that a math equation can be solved if not by you then through someone else. This is natural faith and every man has it. This natural faith engages when seeing Jesus heal miraculously and it causes a person's understanding to open in a new way. After opening, this faith then connects with the faith of Jesus and is not based on what can be heard, seen, touched or felt.

Jesus' faith functions outside the natural five senses and functions from supernatural unseen faith. We receive this kind of faith at our born-again experience.

Jesus's Faith Is Living and Active

It is one thing to believe God can heal the sick and another to put into action Jesus' faith that is within you by actually laying hands on the sick. As you exercise your faith the more confident you'll be in believing people will be healed.

> *It is like a mustard seed which, when it is sown on the ground, is smaller than all the seeds on earth; but when it is sown, it grows up and becomes greater than all herbs, and shoots out large branches, so that the birds of the air may nest under its shade. Mark 4:31-32.*

Note: This isn't saying that your faith is small, this is saying that you will grow into the understanding of faith and learn you can lock into Jesus' faith in you and that you are rooted in Him. The truth is we have to train ourselves to put off the carnal mind that tells us we are lacking something. In Mark 4:31-32, Jesus is encouraging those who feel that their faith is small.

At your born-again experience, you received His portion of faith whether you believe you have faith to move mountains or believe you have little faith. It's not about the measure you think you have. What counts is the measure Christ says you have in Him and what you do with it.

When you activate Jesus' faith in you then you will discover all you have in Christ. Always anchor yourself in His faith and what He has already done. Just do what Holy Spirit instructs you to do and Jesus will do what He promises to do.

It doesn't matter if the person receiving prayer has faith or not. Now, it's nice if they do, but the person receiving is not required to believe in what they don't know as truth. But you have the faith of Jesus within you.

Faith can be visible:

> *And in Lystra a certain man without strength in his feet was sitting, a cripple from his mother's womb, who had never walked. This man heard Paul speaking. Paul, observing him intently and seeing that he had faith to be healed, said with a loud voice, "Stand up straight on your feet!" And he leaped and walked." Acts 14:8-10.*

Paul didn't even have to pray or lay hands on the man, he simply told him to stand up. He understood the power of Jesus' faith within him.

Note: At times, you can literally see faith on people as you talk to them. It's also possible to see faith build up as you share with them, especially after they have encountered a touch from God.

Building up, edifying and encouraging people will open up belief within them as you minister to them. It's important to build faith in those around you. If God gives you a word of prophesy share it. As you do this, you will feel a fire begin to burn in you and you will find yourself growing in the knowledge of Christ in you.

Another way to bring people into faith is by releasing Holy Spirit to flow and create an atmosphere of His presence around those being ministered to. Ask them if they are feeling anything. This can break down preconceived ideas in those you are praying for.

Let's take a look at faith:

> *Now faith is the substance of things hoped for, the evidence of things not seen. Hebrew 11:1.*

So, what is this verse telling us?

- Faith is a substance.
- Faith is things hoped for.
- Faith is evidence.
- Faith functions from the unseen.

Hebrews 12:2 says Jesus is the author of our faith, which means it is His faith. It is not even our faith, it is His faith working in us. At our born again experience we inherit Jesus faith.

> Q: So, if Jesus is faith and he authored faith, who is the substance of faith?
> A: Jesus.
> Q: If Jesus is faith who is our hope?
> A: Jesus.
> Q: So, if Jesus is faith, then who is the evidence of faith?
> A: Jesus.

Let me paraphrase Hebrews 11:1 according to the revelation I received: Now faith is Jesus (substance) of the things hoped for, Jesus is the (evidence) of the unseen realm.

Jesus is faith and He lives in us as the hope of glory. (Colossians 1:27). That means as a believer, the faith of the Son of God dwells in us, empowering us with the ability to function from Jesus's faith. (Galatians 2:20). See without faith (Jesus) it is impossible to please God. So, faith is being sure and confident in the Jesus we hope for and because of Him we are certain of what we don't see.

This is amazing! When we pray for the sick and don't see an instant miracle, we can be certain that what we are not seeing will come to pass.

The Place of Healing in Ministry

1. Jesus wants us to unite as one Spirit in body to do greater works as a whole.

    Truly, truly, I say to you, he who believes in Me, the works that I do, he will do also; and greater works than these he will do; because I go to the Father. John 14:12.

    As you go, proclaim this message: 'The kingdom of heaven has come near.' Heal the sick, raise the dead, cleanse those who have leprosy, drive out demons. Freely you have received; freely give. Matthew 10:7,8.

2. Healing brings people to repentance, this means changing the way they think.

    He got into one of the boats, the one belonging to Simon, and asked him to put out a little from shore. Then he sat down and taught the people from the boat. But when Simon Peter saw it, he fell down at Jesus' knees, saying, "Depart from me, for I am a sinful man, O Lord." For he and all his companions were astonished at the catch of fish they had taken. Luke 5:3,8,9.

3. Miracles reveal God's glory and make people marvel.

But when the multitudes saw it, they marveled, and glorified God, which had given such power unto men. Matthew 9:8.

4. Miracles cause people to believe.

This, the first of his signs, Jesus did at Cana in Galilee, and manifested his glory. And his disciples believed in him. John 2:11.

5. Miracles make people more attentive to God.

And the crowds with one accord paid attention to what was being said by Philip when they heard him and saw the signs that he did. Acts 8:6.

6. Miracles reveal Jesus's identity as the Son of God.

Do you say of Him whom the Father sanctified and said into the world, 'you are blaspheming,' because I said I am the Son of God? If I do not do the works of my Father, do not believe me. But if I do, though you do not believe Me, believe the works that you may know and believe that the Father is in Me, and I in him. John 10:36-38.

7. Miracles reveal the Kingdom of God.

The Lord is good to all: and his tender mercies are over all his works. All thy works shall praise thee, O Lord; and thy saints shall bless thee. They shall speak of the glory of thy kingdom and talk of thy power; To make known to the sons of men his mighty acts, and the glorious majesty of his kingdom. Thy kingdom is an everlasting kingdom, and thy dominion endureth throughout all generations. Psalms 145:9-13.

Points to note:

- Jesus lives in us and we live in Him. (Colossians 3:1-3).

- We function like Jesus in His risen glorified state. (John 14: 12-14).
- Revelation 1:13-15 shows us a portrait of Jesus today in His glorified body living in heaven. At this moment on earth, the Kingdom of God is in you and through you brings the unseen into the seen realm (Matt 10:7).
- The Jesus in you does not doubt, He functions from who He is, faith. (Matthew 21:21).

This leads me to another great point; overcoming doubt.

Overcoming Doubt

Before we embark on this journey to overcome doubt to release faith, we must understand that it is not possible for the new man in us to doubt. Why is this so? It is because Christ in us has recreated us into a new-man through His faith.

So, what is doubt? Doubt is basically the unrewarded logical mind and senses that can be hostile towards God. In the same way Thomas in John 20: 25-28 would only believe unless he saw the physical evidence of Jesus' crucifixion. His logical reasoning was causing doubt within him that the other disciples couldn't have been talking to Jesus. The same thing happens to us in our day. For instance: when you are praying for the sick and the thought crosses your mind, "what if nothing happens?" Overcoming this will require us to ask Holy Spirit, "Is that You talking? Do you think nothing will happen?" But of course, we all know that the Holy Spirit knows something will happen.

The question is who is talking? Is it Jesus? Is it God? No, it is our logic mind creating doubt in us by telling us it won't happen.

The newly created spirit man operates from the mind of the Spirit of Christ thus he is Christ-minded and not carnal minded thinking from old dead man realities. (Colossians 3:1-3).

Thinking like Christ is the key that will help us to understand the thought process of the new man. This will expose the lie of the dead carnal minds perception. Doubt is produced from the untrained senses and logical thinking and not from the new man in whom Jesus, faith, dwells.

Therefore, we can re-define doubt: doubt is the logical/rationale mind telling you a lie, believing it and doing nothing.

If doubts cross your mind, know that these are not your thoughts and in the real sense you are not doubting. You only become doubtful when you choose to entertain carnal mind thoughts which paralyze you into doing nothing.

A double-minded man is someone who knows who they are and what they are capable of but chooses to believe the carnal mind's lie. (James 1:8).

Key points:

- Practice asking Holy Spirit, your teacher, what He thinks of any particular issue or situation. Slowly, you will begin to learn how to put off the natural logic that thinks outside of Spirit and begin growing Christ-minded.
- Christ does not have issues, He has solutions.
- When you're in Christ, you don't have problems, you have promises.
- Renew your mind by changing your thoughts to God's thoughts.

Why must I put off the carnal mind? Because it is not the mind of Christ. The carnal mind can't grasp the things of God and it is hostile towards God. (Rom 8:5-6).

How Do We Learn to Live in The Kingdom of God?

- By training ourselves to think like Christ. The key to discovering Christ is to learn who God is, in us, for us and through us.

- Knowing what Jesus obtained as the Son of God. For example: Christ has the fullness of God in Him. So, you have the fullness of God through Christ. (Colossians 2:9-10). We are in the image and likeness of our Father. It's one thing to know this and another thing to believe in what you know.
- We are like God in Christ. We are not God but we were made in his likeness.
- We are sons, we have the same seed as Jesus, we are identical twins with Jesus.
- In Jesus we have nothing lacking, broken or missing.
- 1 John 4:17: As He is, so are we in this world.

Healing

It's possible some reading this are in need of healing or believing for someone else. You will find keys in this chapter that will help you.

I want to start with a couple of keys that I believe will help. First, we need to learn how to hear from our spirit what Holy Spirit is saying. I know we can hear a lot of different voices; the voice of negative reports, the voice of friends and family, the voice of feelings and emotions, and the voice of your logical mind. Despite the many voices, there is only one voice we need to hear: the voice of Holy Spirit. It is where our faith can birth the faith of Jesus.

Faith is birthed into our natural being through hearing from the Spirit. In reality, we only have one faith and that is the Faith of the Son of God. But our mind and senses need to be trained to live from being one with God and His voice. Our mind and senses are the only part of us that live from a dual perspective that believes there is a division within us. But the truth is that we have been united with Christ and this is the perspective of Jesus.

Listening to what the natural ears and mind are saying will many times contradict and fight against what the spiritual ears are hearing.

Beloved, I pray that you may prosper in all things and be in health, just as your soul prospers. 3 John 2.

We have to train our sensual being and mind to understand that God's will is that we have complete prosperity in Spirit, Soul and Body. For me to properly define prosperity, I have to begin at the heart of it all, which is the Spirit of God. Spiritual prosperity begins within us at our born-again experience. We move from the dead nature into life in Christ. (John 5:24; 1 John 3:14). Spiritually speaking, this means we are transferred from poverty to prosperity.

So, when we talk about prosperity during our salvation experience we are referring to the mind, will, emotions and senses that are being trained and renewed to the mind of the Spirit of God.

> *Receiving the end of your faith—the salvation of your souls. 1 Peter 1:9.*

If we talk about prosperity at an emotional level, this is where we have trained our feelings, senses and renewed them into oneness with the fruit and likeness of the Spirit. When we talk about physical prosperity, we are also talking about walking in health. This is an important revelation that financial prosperity comes to those who are prosperous in their whole being: spirit, soul and body. They have learned that as they train and renew their whole being then they walk in completeness and all of heaven is drawn to them which includes finances.

Let's get an understanding as to what health means. Health is an ongoing state of prosperity of the physical body due to proper care at the natural level. It is a healthy emotional and mental life and a communion with God on a spiritual level. So, if you want to walk in health, you need to know it is a spirit, soul and body issue.

Let's shift gears and talk about healing. Did you know that there are two different kinds of healing that take place? First, God created us in His image which means we too can create. So, that means our body was designed to heal itself. What does that mean? It means we can be healed naturally and, in some cases, we may need medical assistance that will help the body in its natural process of healing. This is amazing and there is nothing wrong with that. Medical assistance helps the body do what God designed it to do. The body is created to fight off organic issues naturally. So, when we are in good health, the body will naturally fight off diseases more effectively. Sad to say, but often the Western diet isn't a healthy lifestyle, so our bodies need aid to naturally fight diseases in the body.

Spiritual healing is the second kind of healing. This is when the Spirit of God manifests in the physical body and brings health and one receives the Spirit of God right into their very cells. In some cases, there can be what scripture calls a spirit of infirmity in a non-believer. It is important to know as a son of God that you only have one Spirit, the Spirit of God. So, a spirit of infirmity is only in a non-believer. I know many would argue that point. But, it's okay and you are entitled to the way you want to interpret that belief.

Divine healing is when the Spirit of God gets into the very cells of your body and drives out whatever is not supposed to be there and brings restoration or even re-creation in the affected area.

When we are believing God to heal we are believing Holy Spirit to move to the affected area and restore it. Or in the case of non-believers, we are to drive out the spirit of infirmity in some cases.

One question I get a lot is how do we walk in divine healing every day? This is a great question with a very simple answer. When one believes, they become one with God: spirit, soul and body. That means when they believe they become one in spirit and that the Spirit of God in them manifests in their body. Simply put, they become the flesh of Jesus' flesh and bone of His bones so when that revelation becomes real to them and they live it out, they will begin to see themselves walk in divine healing every day. But this is a process and takes a lot of renewing of the mind and training the senses into the Truth of God's Word.

My passion is to help you understand the spiritual side of who you are in the Spirit of God. But, if the spiritual doesn't become practical in the natural realm then it won't be effective.

Most people believe in Scripture but fail to understand that their knowledge of the Word isn't belief. But true belief comes from knowing Jesus, the Word, through training our mind and senses and allowing it to become real in our natural day to day life.

Most of the time, believers try to do something without the revelation that it has already been done in the Spirit. They go to extreme measures trying to achieve spiritual things in the flesh without knowing that the works of flesh are dead. The revelation is that they already have what they are trying to believe God for in the natural. So, we have to teach ourselves to tap into the Spirit to learn and receive in the natural the finished work of Christ.

Healing is nothing more than the manifestation of the Spirit of God in our very cells, fiber, tissue and organs of our body. And our cells are responding to the Spirit of God and are removing sickness from our body. That's what healing is, it's simply Holy Spirit invading the sick area.

There are different manifestations of the Spirit of God. There is the omnipresent Spirit according to Psalms 139:7: *"Where shall I go from Your Spirit? Or where can I flee from your presence?"* The Spirit of God is everywhere. Even though we know this we still deal with the issues in the physical instead of the spiritual. So, the question is, does the omnipresent presence of the Spirit heal us? As I thought about this, I began to think about the indwelling Spirit. As born-again believers, we must have the revelation of Who lives inside of us. Most of us know, but do we fully know its reality?

Here is another question for you, do you claim to be filled with the Spirit of God? Ephesians 5:18 says, *"be not drunk with wine in excess but be filled with the Spirit."* If we believe that we are 100 per cent right in our belief and we are filled with the Spirit, does being filled with the Spirit heal us? Being filled with the Spirit doesn't automatically mean our physical body is in health. This is because many of us who are filled with the Spirit of God are focused on our physical issues instead of the Spirit in us. The Spirit of God has literally recreated our spirit-man into the Spirit of God in Christ Jesus. We are a new creation in our spirit-man so we apply it to our physical body.

Then we have something called the manifestation of the Spirit in our flesh or body:

And my speech and my preaching was not with enticing words of man's wisdom but in demonstration of the Spirit and power. 1 Corinthians 2:4.

The revelation here is that the Spirit of God is not just omnipresent or dwelling in us but can bring our physical body into a prosperous state of health. This happens because of the manifestation of the power of the Spirit through a tangible release of the Spirit received at our born-again experience.

Think about this: The Spirit of God moving into the cellular level of your being, invading your body and bringing life to every cell and making them new. I want to challenge you to be heavenly minded. To see things from God's perspective is a practical way of training the mind and senses. Those who walk in divine health release and receive the healing power of the Spirit into their bodies all the time.

Healing can come from the ministry of miraculous healing where someone else comes into agreement and lays hands on people and the Spirit in them manifests in agreement with the spoken Word of God and healing comes. There are those moments of instant miracles and then there are healings that are manifest over time. The important thing to understand is that even if healing takes time, you are still healed. It happened at the moment we received it.

Remember what Mary said to the angel, *"let it be done unto me according to your word."* (Luke 1:38). We need to live in the reality that it is already done. If we don't believe this, then we need to start renewing our minds to the reality that Jesus already did a complete work. Then what are we really trying to accomplish through our confessing and believing? We are simply speaking what our Father is saying. We then align our mind and senses to the reality of the Spirit of God.

Then there are times the Word of God comes alive and it's like an open heaven becoming more real to you than ever before.

There are so many ways the manifestation of healing can come to a believer. There are times healing ministers may say: "I feel or I sense this or that," and when they lay hands on the person they are healed. Again, the moment we believe in our spirit that we are healed is key. If I lay hands on you for example after you are healed, it means I'm in agreement with the finished work and sometimes uniting faith can bring instant healing or speed up the process.

We can discern what God is doing through our feelings but only when we learn the feelings of the Lord. If not, then our senses can easily be misinterpreted as God but it is only our senses grounded in the flesh. But I believe we can train our mind and senses, feelings and emotions to the point we can learn to trust our feelings and emotions in Christ.

What happens during healing is that the Spirit of God transfers from us into them, or their Spirit unites with our Spirit and the united transfer of God's Spirit creates a healing explosion. When we allow the Spirit to move into our natural body and help it do what it was created to do, healing is manifested. At this point I'm guessing the question we may be asking ourselves is how do we let the Spirit move in us to manifest healing? How does the Spirit move into the pain and sickness that the body is facing?

I want to start by looking at our role model Jesus. Scripture tells us to be imitators of God. (Ephesians 5:1-2). Jesus was filled with the Spirit of God and worked great miracles. So, we too, being full of Holy Spirit, can release the same healing power that Jesus released into those in need of healing.

Romans 8:11 tells us that the Spirit quickens our mortal bodies. I know many people believe that this has to do with being raised up in the last day. But I don't think this verse is talking about a resurrected body but instead is talking about the physical body. Why? Because later in Romans, the Bible uses the term mortal bodies to tell us not to let sin reign in it.

The Scripture above is talking about this body we live in now. It says, He who was raised from the dead will quicken your mortal body with His Spirit that dwells in you. The Spirit dwelling in us has more than one purpose: to quicken us. That means to heal us by going into our flesh to bring life. It also means to remove anything that is not supposed to be there.

Here is an example: Say we have a disease in our body. When healing takes place the Spirit of God moves within our body and removes the infirmity. The Spirit also quickens us and this includes our tissues, cells, pains, joints, basically every part of us.

But how? When the Spirit of Jesus touches our bodies, He deposits His Spirit. Mark 6:56 says that *"as many as touched Him were made whole."* When the flesh of man touches the Spirit it literally manifests in man's flesh. This is one-way Jesus was delivering the Spirit into their bodies. It is important to know that they were not becoming born again but that they were getting healed. The body/flesh was being touched by the Spirit of God.

Matthew 8:8 says that the Word of God is a delivery system for the Spirit into the flesh. Didn't Jesus say His words are Spirit and life? What does the Spirit do to our mortal bodies? It quickens or gives life to us and we can use this on any level of our spirit, soul and or body. (John 6:63). Another scripture is that the Word is medicine to our bodies. (Proverbs 4:22). When the Word is spoken, it will impact the body to bring health.

We find in John 9:7 that obedience is a delivery system for the Word of God. The man mentioned in this verse heard the Word, obeyed it and accessed the miracle. So, obedience to the Word activated it to come to life and caused it to work on his eyes and he received his sight.

Another delivery system of God's is through hearing. (Luke 5:15). Romans 10:17 says that *"faith comes by hearing the Word of God."* A lot of things manifest through hearing. Belief comes by hearing. But then, fear, depression, worry, and stress also come by hearing. There are two ways of hearing, one is through our natural fleshly ears and secondly, our spiritual ears. Right now, you are reading this and your natural ears are listening. But you also have spiritual ears and it is from there your faith is activated. So whatever ears you're hear from will either release a natural fleshly faith or cause the Faith of the Son of God to be activated. If a doctor gives a bad report, we will hear with our natural ears creating faith in the doctor's report which produces worry, fear, and stress. But if we hear with spiritual ears, the Faith of the Son of God speaks power, love and a sound mind that then activates the Spirit into the natural body and heals it. Any healing that I have witnessed is the result of listening from the ears of the Spirit and obeying.

Amos 3:3 says, *"how can two walk together unless they agree?"* Then how can we walk in divine health if we don't come into agreement with the Word of God? We must come into unity with the mind of the Spirit of Christ and walk in agreement with His truth to see the manifestation in our life regardless of feelings, emotion and thinking. Even now as you are reading this, you will begin to experience the Spirit moving through your body.

The creative spoken Word of life is a delivery system. (Luke 4:39). Notice how we speak is will deliver the Spirit into someone's body. Scripture says life and death is in the power of the tongue. When we speak, the cells and tissues and body parts come into alignment with our spoken creative word. The spoken word turns around everything that is wrong and makes it right. There are many other delivery systems even outside of what I'm sharing with you now. I just want to open your mind to the Mind and Eyes of the Spirit and from there you can explore.

How do you get what is in our Spirit to manifest into our body? Just speak and command imperatively like Jesus did. It brings glory to the Father when we use and exercise the gifts and promises He has given to us.

We find in Luke 4:40 that the laying on of hands is a delivery method. Laying your hands on someone transfers the Spirit into their body. This can happen with believers and non-believers. Some people might be walking in a greater level of faith because they have probably grown in the understanding of all they have in Jesus. But then another is still growing and discovering that when they pray for people they can unite and stir-up the faith of the believer as well as non-believers even if they don't believe. Either way the Spirit of God gets into them.

Mark 11:24 says that believing is a delivery method. I want you to notice how God is making this as easy as possible for us. For example, He says believe and you will receive. There is a big difference between believing with our spirit and believing with the mind. It's with the heart or spirit that man believes unto salvation. Salvation is for the whole person; physically and spiritually. The reason many believers struggle with healing is because they are trying to make it happen with their carnal minds instead of through the Spirit. It is not in what we can touch, feel, see or hear.

The things we have been told we will receive from God when we die and go to heaven is actually ours now. We already have it so we cannot earn or achieve it on our own.

Like we have said, there are so many ways to minister healing. Sickness can be deep in the heart, in the physical or mental parts of a person Simple acts of love can bring healing to a world that is groaning for God's manifest love.

Think about a person in a wheel chair. Most people only see the physical, but what do you think that person is experiencing in his heart? The pain in within can be a place that requires healing as much if not more than the physical healing.

When Jesus died on the cross He healed, set free, delivered and made us whole. What part of us did Jesus heal?

Often, when we are asked this question, our mind turns quickly to the physical body. We think Jesus died only to heal our bodies. But think about this. Could He have died to bring our body into reconciliation with the Father? What did He die for? Now when I say this I know you are thinking about the physical and spiritual. Scripture tells us we are not flesh but spirit.

> *But you are not in the flesh but in the Spirit, if indeed the Spirit of God dwells in you. Now if anyone does not have the Spirit of Christ, he is not His. Romans 8:9.*

So, who did Jesus die for to bring back into right standing with the Father? What part of you is born again? It's your spirit that is 100% healed, whole, set free and delivered. (John 3:5). It's the Spirit of God who brings spiritual healing to you. This brings your soul and body into alignment with your born-again spirit.

It is part of our training to renew our logical thinking into the Spirit's perspective so we don't find ourselves building scripture around a false perspective, creating a fleshly/soul-minded belief system. Our natural man governed by the Spirit will walk in completeness and wholeness. (1Thessalonians 5:23).

Key points:

- We have been made whole, complete and perfected in spirit, soul and body.
- Healing is rooted in and flows from our core.
- Our physical healing comes from the Spirit of Christ Jesus in us. (Colossians 1:27).

I know you are going to ask, "What about my physical and emotional pain?" This question is why in our Sonship Lifestyle Trainings, we don't teach people how to heal the sick. Instead we teach our students New Covenant realities, helping each to discover the inheritance already dwelling in them. (1 Corinthians 2:12). From there they will manifest all they need.

Revelation

Revelation is key in becoming connected with who we are as New Covenant sons. It is God's way of keeping us connected to our right mind, the mind of Christ, and His thoughts and heart's desire for us. When a believer gains understanding and gets hold of the truth of their kingdom authority then healing and gifts of the Spirit can be ministered in many creative ways.

Here is some creative ways Jesus and the apostles used to heal the sick:

- Touch
- From a distance
- Finger in ears
- Spit in the eyes
- Spit on the tongue
- Spit, mud balls and action
- One word of deliverance: "go"
- Faith
- Oil
- Shadows
- Cloths
- Edge of a cloak
- Pronouncement and declarations
- Word of command

I've personally seen many healed through prophetic words.

Remember the sky is the limit with possibilities. Just listen to the Holy Spirit and have fun, be creative.

Let's look at two types of healing prayer we can engage in:

- Petitioning prayer – Example: "God please heal this person." It's a bit like asking our boss to do a job that we have been given to do. God has already delegated His authority to us to go heal the sick. Remember we don't function from earth to heaven, we function from our home and throne as kings in heaven to earth. Jesus or the disciples never used petitioning prayer for healing but instead prayed in agreement with the Spirit of God.
- Commanding Prayer: Example- "issue be gone or be healed". This is exercising our delegated authority from the Father.

  And Jesus said unto them, Because of your unbelief: for verily I say unto you, if ye have faith as a grain of mustard seed, ye shall say unto this mountain, 'Remove hence to yonder place'; and it shall remove; and nothing shall be impossible unto you. Matthew 17:20 (KJV).

Healing prayer comes from the authority given us from knowing all things are possible.

Points to Think About:

- Sometimes, a word of encouragement that builds up and edifies or a prophetic word or a word of knowledge, can bring healing and set people free. As spiritual sons of God and as a new creation we have life within us to be manifested through love.
- Many people are worried and overwhelmed by the hustles and bustles of life's stresses. A word that produces life can change the atmosphere and bring peace, joy and love into the lives of those we encounter.
- Another powerful way to touch lives is to simply love on people through taking time to listen. The art of listening is powerful. I'm convinced that the body of Christ needs to master the skill of listening without having to give a response.

Practical Tool:

In your next conversation, listen to the person talking without giving a reply or solution. Train your mind to not think of a reply and teach it to listen attentively. When you do respond, respond with a question to keep the person talking. This is a tool for practicing self-control and mastering the art of listening.

Walking in Divine Healing

Jesus commissioned all believers to heal:

> *Then Jesus came up and said to them, All authority in heaven and on earth has been given to me. Therefore, go and make disciples of all nations, baptizing them in the name of the Father and the Son and the Holy Spirit, teaching them to obey everything I have commanded you. And remember, I am with you always, to the end of the age. Matthew 28:18-20 (NET Bible).*

What did Jesus command the Disciples to do?

> *As you go, preach this message: 'The kingdom of heaven is near!' Heal the sick, raise the dead, cleanse lepers, cast out demons. Freely you received, freely give. Do not take gold, silver, or copper in your belts, no bag for the journey, or an extra tunic, or sandals or staff, for the worker deserves his provisions. Matthew 10:7-10*

First Jesus sent out the twelve with authority over every sickness, disease and evil spirit:

> *Jesus called his twelve disciples and gave them authority over unclean spirits so they could cast them out and heal every kind of disease and sickness. Matthew 10:1.*

Then Jesus sent out the seventy-two with the same authority:

> *Heal the sick in that town and say to them, 'The kingdom of God has come upon you!' Luke 10:9.*

> *Then the seventy-two returned with joy, saying, "Lord, even the demons submit to us in your name!" So, he said to them, "I saw Satan fall like lightning from heaven. Look, I have given you authority to tread on snakes and scorpions and on the full force of the enemy, and nothing will hurt you. Nevertheless, do not rejoice that the spirits submit to you, but rejoice that your names stand written in heaven. Luke 10:17-20.*

Healing wasn't just given to the disciples alone; it is for every believer in Christ.

The authority that Jesus was given is the same authority He has given to us! This authority is mission focused. No matter what you have been called to do you have also been commissioned with authority by Jesus to go heal the sick. (Matthew 28:18 tells us that all authority has been given to Jesus and in Luke 10:19 we read that Jesus has given us authority.)

In Colossians 1:19, Apostle Paul tells us that the Father was pleased to have all His fullness dwell in Jesus and Colossians 2:9 says, *"for in him dwells all the fullness of the Godhead bodily."*

I want you to understand that through Jesus the fullness of the Godhead now lives in you. It is a free gift.

Think about this for a moment. When you receive a gift, it becomes yours. You become the owner of that gift. Likewise, we have been given gifts as sons of God and it is time we took ownership of our gifts and know who we are in Christ.

> *And thus, to know the love of Christ that surpasses knowledge, so that you may be filled up to all the fullness of God. Ephesian 3:19.*

In our discovery of who Jesus is in us, for us, and through us, we learn of the fullness of God in us. That means you are lacking nothing because you have Jesus who is everything in you.

We train our body/flesh and mind to align with who we are in the Spirit, our true identity. As sons and daughters, we speak from our spirit into the soul and body to line up with who we are in the Spirit.

Healing Is God's Love in Action

Love should be our motivation for going out into the marketplace to share our faith. We should be compelled by love. Whether instant healing happens or not, the people you encounter should be left with no doubt that God loves them and that Jesus died for them. Make sure to always treat them with the utmost respect, dignity, gentleness, kindness and love. At all times God desires to reveal his love through you.

Key Note: Love and Compassion is our motivation for healing the sick and prophesying.

For the love of Christ compels us; because we thus judge, that if one died for all, then were all dead. 2 Corinthians 5:14 (KJV).

Jesus was always moved with love and compassion for others. Matthew 14:14 says, *"And Jesus went forth, and saw a great multitude, and was moved with compassion toward them, and he healed their sick"* (KJV).

Love and compassion moved Jesus to heal the sick.

And Jesus, moved with compassion, put forth his hand, and touched him, and saith unto him, I will; be thou clean. Mark 1:41(KJV).

Further John 11:32-35 says:

Then when Mary was come where Jesus was, and saw him, she fell down at his feet, saying unto him, Lord, if thou hadst been here, my brother had not died. When Jesus therefore saw her weeping, and the Jews also weeping which came with her, he groaned in the spirit, and was troubled. And said, where have ye laid him? They said unto him, Lord, come and see. Jesus wept. (KJV).

In this passage Jesus was not late, He was on God's time. See, the resurrection that took place was not about the event but about the fact that resurrection power was Jesus.

Ask your teacher, Holy Spirit, to give you greater understanding of the Father's love and compassion. We all need this on a daily basis and especially when we are laying hands on the sick and prophesying.

How Healing Manifests

We believe that God can heal every sickness, pain, crippling disease or deformity and that He can even create body parts, dissolve implanted metal and plastic and turn them into bone and flesh. We are to believe God can bring life to the dead. We are also not afraid to acknowledge that some people do not get instant manifestations of physical healing. For instance, the 10 lepers Jesus prayed for received their healing as they went.

So how does healing come, and what do you say and do when there is no instant sign of healing?

I encourage you not to use these words: "I guarantee or promise", unless the Holy Spirit tells you otherwise. However, I do use the words sometimes, but do avoid saying things like "you are healed" until the person has confirmed the healing. It's easier to walk someone through the process of them seeing their healing manifest in the near future. The people you are ministering to will either be instantly healed, experience partial or gradual healing, or have no sign of healing. It's important for us to find out which one of these three they are experiencing.

Note: We know they are healed but until it manifests in the physical don't leave them confused as to why you are saying they are healed yet they are still in pain. Most people are busy and, on the move, and you won't have time to explain the process and details of why you believe they are healed but they are still in pain.

I recommend that you save yourself the explanation and just love on the people you are ministering to and let Holy Spirit do His work in their life. I hope this makes sense. Again, it is not a lack of belief to not say, "you are healed or I guarantee". You are dealing with carnal minded people who may not understand, whether they are believers or non-believers, and who may not know fully what you have inside you. So, let your actions speak louder than words.

Note: If you like, you can leave them with your Facebook or email and they can connect with you and you can answer their questions later.

Analyzing What Could Happen When You Pray for Healing:

1. Instant healing manifestation:

When you have commanded the issue to go, the person most of the time will be healed instantly. Always ask the person to test and check whether they are healed or whether the pain they had is gone. Do this immediately after agreeing in a commanding prayer. Obviously for some it may mean a trip to the doctor to confirm the healing. But the moment they say there is no pain or the issue is gone; at that point you can say God healed you.

2. Partial healing:

People may experience various degrees of healing and you can say to them: "God is up to something special in your life." Why? Because their healing can come as they go, it can become noticeable in 15 minutes, a day, a week or month from the time you commanded healing. This is a great time to give your contact information and say you would like to explain how healing works. To let them know you are there for them if they need more agreement in prayer." If you are part of a local church, let them know where you worship, time and place. Always leave them with hope and a way to connect with you or someone.

3. No sign of healing

Two things happen at this point:

- There is no sign that they have been healed but as they go they get healed. They can find out a day or more later that they have been healed; or gradual healing takes place after they leave.
- When you have prayed and there is no sign of healing and no change in their condition at all afterward.

This is what I say in such a situation: "If you haven't seen instant manifestation of healing right now, it's not a sign that God doesn't love you or care about you or that you are not going to be healed. God loves you and is passionate about you." We let them know that sometimes they can experience

Gods healing later. I use the 10 lepers as an example of those Jesus prayed for who received their healing after they went on their way.

Note: If they don't experience any change in their condition, tell them to contact you for more prayer.

Keep them encouraged and edified. I can't lie, sometimes people never get healed physically. I know the big question is why don't they see a manifestation of healing? I can't answer that question fully; all I can say is if we try to figure it out, we could end up having to re-write the truth about God's word to make it fit the situation we are facing.

I encourage you to not try figuring it out, just know that you are doing what Jesus commissioned you to do. Stand on the Truth and know there is no other way for a son to think.

Now let me say I have seen these same people so touched by God's love that they give their lives to Him. Sometimes people don't care unless they know how much you care for them. Always remember this is happening from the place of love and compassion.

I often ask the Holy Spirit to teach me how to steward what He has placed in me. Learning how to steward this gift when believers see someone on their death bed rise up and walk and the crowds are pushing in on you. Then to steward well His gift when I pray for someone on their death bed and they die. If you are not secure in your identity and inheritance in Christ, this will shake your senses and logical mind because you will question God and yourself. We must train our reasoning faculties to become settled in what God said is the truth and just know you did what you were told and trust God for the rest.

CHAPTER FOUR

THE ROLE OF HOLY SPIRIT

The Holy Spirit in you attracts all of heaven and earth towards you. You lack nothing, you are limitless and you can do all things through Him who dwells in you. He is your life coach. He partners with you in love, peace, joy, self-control and in comfort. The times you're troubled Holy Spirit is there as your Comforter and He will help you.

Here Are Some of The Ways Holy Spirit Functions in You:

Peace: Jesus in you, the hope of glory, is the Prince of Peace. "As you go" daily you are an instrument and a vessel. The very essence of God's peace dwells in you. Wherever your foot treads, you create an atmosphere of hope and safety——an oasis where people can find rest and peace that surpasses all human understanding. You have a peace in you that the world is yearning for. (John 14:27).

Gentleness: The world is full of broken, wounded and hurting people from either past experiences or current situations and relationships. Many have been let down by other Christians and even the church. This is where we allow the world to see what the sonship lifestyle looks like through pure gentleness and love.

> *He does not fight nor shout; He does not raise his voice in the streets! He does not crush the weak or quench the smallest hope; He will end all conflict with his final victory, and His name shall be the hope of all the world. Matthew 12:19-21 (TLB).*

Love: The compassionate love of Jesus propels us out of our comfort zone. The people we encounter daily should always be left with no doubt that God loves them. Whether they get healed when we pray for them or not, they should encounter God's love. The important thing is for people to encounter the Spirit of God and His passionate love for them.

Compassion: As sons/ daughters of God, we function as Christ did. Jesus was continually moved with compassion. (Matthew 9:36). Jesus had compassion for the lost, hurting, and broken. Compassion is in the heart of the Spirit of God and it comes out of us through acts of love and words that build up, encourage and edify. We all need Jesus' compassion. Compassion is the power behind healings and miracles.

Leadership: As a son of God, you have the nature of a leader in you. Holy Spirit will lead you into all truth because He is a great leader and brings the leader out in you. The Spirit of Jesus Christ in you turns you into the pure, perfect likeness and image of your Father. If Holy Spirit is a leader by nature, so what does that make you?

> *You have the nature of the King of Kings dwelling inside you. Your spirit is born into royalty. (1 Peter 2:9).*

That means the Spirit of Jesus in you has the fullness of all leadership qualities that you need to lead. We have all these things bestowed in us. We are in the process of learning and growing into our kingship as we submit our minds and become renewed in the nature of the Spirit. A true leader talks and acts like the King of Kings who is their role model. In other words, we become imitators of God. My goal is to pull the leader out of you.

Often leadership is misunderstood as management. But I am talking about something different here. A true leader builds up, edifies, encourages, inspires, motivates and leads people into their destiny, purpose and plan. A leader is there for the people around them to succeed.

The Spirit of God in you qualifies you as a leader. It is important that we take ownership of who the Father is in us, for us and through us. Leadership qualities manifest through you on the streets, workplace, school or marketplace. As you live life as a son of God you will see so many lives changed simply because of who the Father is in you. A leader is a person of influence just like God, Holy Spirit and Jesus.

There are four things we can do to have an impact on people:

- Become a role model. Everyone has someone who looks up to them. Believe it or not, someone is looking up to you right now.
- Learn to influence, motivate, encourage and edify people.
- Become a trainer. This is what I like to call discipleship. There are two ministries that should be a part of every believer; one is the ministry of reconciliation and the other is discipleship. Every believer has been commissioned to do this.
- Multiply. This means increasing in number and especially the number of believers. Very few Christians are at this point. As we reach out to non-believers, our aim is to multiply the Kingdom of God.

I like to summarize the above points as **RIOTS**!

Role model
Influence
Overcome
Train others
Send

My passion is to start kingdom **RIOTS** everywhere I go.

Most people get stuck in their walk with Christ because we don't have enough people role modeling the Jesus lifestyle. Too many leaders tell, but few shows how it is done.

Teaching others by being a role model is important so that they too can learn to walk through all the stages. So many people never reach the stage of training and sending. To be honest, many people struggle to learn how to influence or overcome in life. This little tool will help you become the born leader that you are in the Spirit.

A leader is given responsibility from Father God as he matures in his journey as a son. Let's say you have two sons and one of them wants to be like you and so he follows you around and imitates everything that you do. This son does things in the exact same way you do and for the same purpose.

When he comes of age, you are confident to give him the keys to your car because you know he will drive the car as you do and use it in the same way that you do. The son does this because he wants to be like you. He might make a few mistakes but you know it is okay because you want him to manage/govern what you have as his father.

As for your other son, you love him equally but he does not really care or show interest in what you do. All he wants to do are his own things. But you don't mind because you still love him. However, when he is of age, he cannot have the car. Even if the car is his inheritance and belongs to him, he cannot have it because he will hurt himself.

This is exactly how God works with us. As sons though we own everything, we are still in training into the kingship of the King of Kings. We are still under the tutorship of Holy Spirit who is training us to steward what we carry.

We have been born into the kingdom. You are perfect and you are the title deed carrier to all that the kingdom has to offer including the things that you don't even know that you own.

Holy Spirit is teaching us to live out a lifestyle of Jesus. As we become more and more like Him we govern our senses through the Spirit's reality which opens up access to all that is ours. It is important to note that it is not something you earn, but it's a gift and God desires you to take responsibility and steward it faithfully.

Great leaders are always stepping into a greater maturity as a son. I want you to capture the importance of learning to be a leader. Everyone can learn to be a leader, in varying degrees, even though you might not think you were born with it.

Prophecy

We all know Jesus and Holy Spirit are interceding for us. As we also learned earlier, the two are talking about us day and night. Could prophecy be what They are saying about us?

What are they saying about you? What is Jesus saying about you? What is the Holy Spirit saying about you? What are they saying about everyone else? How does God see you? What does God think about you? Why are Their thoughts about us important? It is because Their thoughts are heaven/kingdom thoughts. Knowing about God's thoughts concerning us is the point where God unlocks the doors of our mind to encounter the unfathomable treasures of our identity as Spirit sons of God.

My goal isn't to just give you information. Prophesy isn't just about the mechanics of it but in understanding how God sees prophesy, why we need it and how it can help people. Prophesy flows from a lot of personal time with the Holy Spirit. We need to tap into what They are saying. This is the heart beat of prophesy.

People connect in different ways but I do it through journaling. I ask Holy Spirit a lot of questions and I write down what He is saying. Learning to hear what God is saying is what prophesy is. Your approach and delivery are the same as healing the sick.

So, in this section, I'm going to show you how prophesy impacts lives just like healing does, possibly greater in many cases. This is because not everyone needs a healing but there's not one person who doesn't want to know what God is saying. Allow me to share a couple of illustrations and then I trust Holy Spirit will help you grow in this first step.

Before we begin I want to challenge you to read the book of Revelation. Don't try to understand it but read and pay attention to Apostle John's relationship with Jesus. John considered himself Jesus' best friend. So, watch how Jesus allows him to see and hear from Him. The sole purpose was to bless the body of Christ then and today. Prophesying is about building up, edifying and encouragement.

I have learned so much from reading the book of Revelation and watching the dialogue between Jesus and John.

I always ask God to give me the ability to see what He sees. This is because prophesy isn't only speaking what God says but it's also seeing what God sees. When you train yourself in this way you will start to see people in a different way.

I believe there is something God wants us to see in Genesis 1:1. Everything God did He spoke it into existence with His words. The Bible describes the beginning of the earth as empty and lifeless, having no substance and full of darkness. The darkness also means there was no vision or sight. Then God does something; He speaks what was in His imagination. God's solution to the darkness and void in the earth was to say what He saw and then it was.

Children of God are crying out for more. They desire to go deeper into the things of the Spirit. God's people want more and they think they will find it in an event but in reality, they need a deeper relationship with Christ and discovering the Jesus in them.

Again, in Genesis, we see the Spirit of God hovering over the empty place and His very presence starts to deposit something into the atmosphere. God deposits His spoken word, "Let there be light." He literally speaks light into being. What God did was to release what was inside Himself and deposited it on the earth. Therefore, God's answer to emptiness and darkness is His own substance, His light.

His light becomes the answer to filling the void or the lack of resources. Light becomes the answer to darkness and absence of sight.

All of this is in the power of the Word. Who is the Word? Jesus.

See, this world we live in is crazy with chaos in many areas such as finances, relationships and spirituality. But with the power of God's spoken word, we can bring all things into His light.

God can use us to speak from our being, where Jesus dwells, into someone's life. One word can change the worst of situations and hold things that are falling apart together for His glory.

This is the beautiful part of the prophetic word, it brings God's glory into the seen realm.

So, when people who are experiencing certain unsettling situations in their lives come to us, they do so because of Who is in us. The One in us is Christ, the hope of glory.

When we speak a prophetic word to someone, we are actually speaking the power and presence of God into that person's life. We are releasing heaven into them through our words. We can therefore confidently say that as sons of God, we are His hovering, physical presence on earth.

In the Garden of Eden, everything started with the presence of God. So, we need that presence and to hear what He's saying. But why? It's because the world is groaning and longing for a manifestation of God. Because God is within us we can help those who are longing for an encounter with Him.

When the faith of God in us comes to life, the unseen becomes seen through kingdom encounters. Healing takes place, prophesies are spoken, dreams are interpreted and many other miracles take place. Prophetic words counter darkness, emptiness and chaos.

People may lack opportunity and resources, but one word from God can bring opportunities where they did not exist before. How you might ask? Because when God said the word the opportunity was created and it was enabled to manifest. God's prophetic word will release the opportunity and the opportunity will release resources.

Releasing strategic prophetic words helps people see how everything fits together and how to get to where they want to be in life.

Chaos and lack throws our lives into dysfunction but a prophetic word may bring order. The prophetic word allows us to see what God sees and then it fills the emptiness. One strategic word can accelerate progress within us and open doors. This can come through scripture, prayer, personal prophecy or an interpretation of a dream that can literally birth an idea in us.

Note that in Genesis 1, God did not look at the void and darkness and say, "That looks pretty messed up and is going to take a lot to clean it up". No. He simply said, "Let there be light!" The same thing applies to our lives. When God speaks He doesn't condemn but He speaks light and order. He brings a solution to our craziness and mess.

Prophesies bring solutions to the issues of life. As Prophetic people we are not called to identify the problem, but to release people into their full potential in Christ. (1 Timothy 1:18).

People often ask why they see the problem or the negative side of people? My answer is simple: God shows you the problem, the void, so you can speak solution to the problem through God's light. Holy Spirit will show you the diagnosis (problem) so you can give the prognosis (solution). But just because you see the problem does not mean you need to respond to it but rather respond from the Answer, Jesus in us the Hope of Glory.

Let us make this more practical by looking at John 1:43-50. This passage shows us the prophetic word of knowledge at work and paints a picture of Jesus moving through the gifts of the Holy Spirit effortlessly. When getting words of knowledge, you get pictures, impressions or visions. I'd like you to notice how Jesus does this in a conversation. We see Jesus talking to Nathaniel who seems to be a spiritual skeptic. However, Jesus turns him into a believer through discernment.

Discernment isn't only about knowing people's problems. Nine out of ten people say it is about knowing what is evil. That is true at times because we need to be able to discern good from evil or discern whether there are evil spirits present.

But what does discern actually mean? It means distinguishing between breaths. Where is the first place the Bible talks about breath?

The first place is in the book of Genesis during the creation of Adam. God breathed into man and gave him life. And God did not just give man life alone when He breathed into him. He also breathed His very nature into him. So, each person has a unique breath of God breathed into them. So, one of the manifestations of discernment is in distinguishing the breath of God that's in each individual. Our job as a prophetic people is to discern whether they have the nature of God in them.

When God breathed into man, He put the breath of heaven, His breath, inside man. This is what Jesus did with Nathaniel in John 1:47. Jesus refers to Nathaniel as a true Israelite in whom there is nothing false. Jesus recognizes the Spirit of God in him. Nathaniel was a skeptic, but Jesus turned something that seemed dark into light.

Sometimes we back down when a person we are trying to minister to responds with disbelief. But like Jesus, you can turn it around into something positive. We do not want to prejudge people because of their initial response because we don't want our attitude to turn them away. We can choose not to react to them according to the spirit in them, but according to the way God sees them. Be careful not to miss an opportunity due to the way someone responds or their attitude towards you. Always remember people can pick up on your vibe or your attitude.

When Jesus responded to Nathaniel, He told him he was the kind of guy who lives the truth. He didn't point out his skepticism but focused on what God saw in him. We must follow Christ's example.

Hearing God

Understanding how to hear God entails coming to the place where you learn who God is for us. It is discovering what God and His image is like. This is not meant to be an answer to anything specific but should cause us to go deeper into discovering who God is in us. Jesus came to paint a picture of God the Father. He literally put a physical face on God. (John 1:18). So, we as sons take on the fullness of the Godhead through Christ. Jesus said something profound when He said that "if you have seen Me, you have seen the Father."

So, what is God like? We need to really think about this because to capture this we must break past the surface of what we have been told and delve into the Spirit to discover this. The key is in understanding the Gospel. Think about this: what did Jesus come to say and do? He came to set the captives free and to talk about blessings and favor.

When you read Luke 4:14-21, you see the purpose and calling of Jesus. This scripture really paints a portrait of Jesus, His purpose and identity, and what He was known for. Jesus was manifested to bring grace and goodness. The Bible says he went about doing good and healing all who were oppressed of the devil. (Acts 10:38). So, what is the Gospel? It's the good news of what God is really like.

There is an important thing that is not taught in many Christian circles and that is learning how God sees Himself. If we don't know how God sees Himself then we cannot understand how God sees us. In Exodus 33:18-23, Moses asked God to show Him His glory and He agreed. He told Moses, *"I will cause my goodness to pass before you."* So, God tucked Moses in the cleft of the rock and covered him with His hand. Moses got a rear-end view of God. From this we have a full-frontal view of God and all of His goodness and grace. As you read this passage, see what God says about Himself because that is the identity and the heart of God. This is the first time in scripture that God talks about Himself. Here the Father is talking about His goodness, graciousness and mercy. He reveals His attributes.

How we know God and how we see Him becomes a basis of how we hear from Him. Our testimony becomes the reality of how God desires to speak to us. For me, my testimony is that God is the kindest person I have ever met in my life. He has been persistent in His goodness, love and mercy towards me over the years. The beautiful thing about God is that we can never mistake where we are with Him. Why? Because God never changes, He is always the same. So, what I'm saying is that the way He presents Himself to us and the way He makes Himself known to us never changes. His love, grace, mercy and goodness remain the same.

Let's talk about something else. Can we make God happy or sad? If our answer is yes then it suggests that we can manipulate His mood. But think about that for a second. Can you really control God or His feelings about us? These are things we need to overcome in order to live in the victory that is already ours. God's thoughts about us are not built around our behavior. Our performance can change but our performance doesn't change God. See, God's approach to us isn't dependent on our approach to Him. Everything with God is based solely on who God is, His faithfulness and Who He will always be.

So, any voice that condemns, accuses, judges or is angry is not the voice of God because the Scripture does not mention them as attributes of God. Any prophetic word must be in agreement with the Gospel. God's love never changes. The work of Holy Spirit is to help us discover God's goodness and kindness and to learn the height, depth, length and breadth of God's love towards us. So, the voice that speaks and draws you to feel and experience these attributes is the voice of God. It is a key component to understand that the voice of God is founded in His nature.

The voice of God will always allow us to know what He feels about us, even when we make mistakes. Learning to hear God's voice can be hard at first because the logical mind will play tricks on us. But we must learn to relax, be at rest and pay close attention to the voice speaking of who God is.

The carnal mind will seldom say anything kind about God, His nature and His goodness. The carnal mind will condemn us and speak vile things about us. Apostle Paul teaches on this in Colossians 3:5-15:

> *Put to death therefore what is earthly in you: sexual immorality, impurity, passion, evil desire, and covetousness, which is idolatry. On account of these the wrath of God is coming. In these you too once walked, when you were living in them. But now you must put them all away: anger, wrath, malice, slander, and obscene talk from your mouth. Do not lie to one another, seeing that you have put off the old self with its practices and have put on the new self, which is being renewed in knowledge after the image of its creator. Here there is not Greek and Jew, circumcised and*

uncircumcised, barbarian, Scythian, slave, free; but Christ is all, and in all. Put on then, as God's chosen ones, holy and beloved, compassionate hearts, kindness, humility, meekness, and patience, bearing with one another and, if one has a complaint against another, forgiving each other; as the Lord has forgiven you, so you also must forgive. And above all these put-on love, which binds everything together in perfect harmony. And let the peace of Christ rule in your hearts, to which indeed you were called in one body. And be thankful.

What I want us to see in this Scripture are the attributes of the dead man and the carnal mind. Next, observe how the attributes of the new man function in the likeness of the Father. Knowing this will help you distinguish the voice talking to you and help you clearly define the voice of God.

So, let's analyze the voice of God. The voice of God speaks what is good, compassionate, loving and kind. His voice brings peace and bears with our mistakes and is always forgiving. God's voice will always make you feel secure. His voice shows and demonstrates His attributes.

Grace is God's voice enabling us to remain firm even if we stumble. We are all learning at every stage of our lives. The voice that speaks to you in peace, rest and kindness is the voice we should listen to.

Here are some keys to know when God is speaking to you:

- Learn to listen from the new heart which is (The Spirit) in you and not from your own understanding or mind.
- Become a student yearning to learn about the nature of God. The more you get acquainted with His nature and mindset, the more you will know when God is speaking to you.
- Become a person who listens more than talks in your prayer life. Have moments of quietness and attentively listening to God without being in a hurry.

The same way God speaks and connects with us will be the way we will connect and influence others. So, always look for that kind, loving and gentle voice even while it is correcting us. You won't come away from prayer feeling guilty and ashamed. In the end we will be thankful to God for helping us discover who we are in Him.

God will always be straight forward and tell you the truth. But He does it in a way that sets us free and not put us in condemnation and fear. He tells us the truth so that we can become like the Truth He is. Remember God gave us a new heart. So, we must listen from that heart and nature of God within us. The voice of God speaks to us in a way that edifies, builds, stirs and encourages us.

APPENDIX A:

MARKETPLACE MINISTRY DO'S AND DON'TS

The healing ministry takes place in a loving and compassionate atmosphere that is full of the presence and the power of the Holy Spirit.

Follow these steps of approach:

1. Introduce yourself and those with you. If possible, men should pray with men and women with women.
2. Ask the person for their name and remember to use it while you are talking to them. This is a great exercise to help you remember names. Always pray with respect, dignity, gentleness, kindness, and love.

Always ask for permission to pray for someone and to lay hands on them. Use discernment if you see they are uncomfortable. If they are uneasy point out to them where you want to touch them and wait for their approval. If they still don't want you to touch them that is okay because God can heal them anyway.

Always use authoritative prayer when praying for the sick. Don't slip back into petitioning God. Petitioning prayers are good when you are using them to lift the person to God, but not when you are ministering healing.

It's good to have company when you are out ministering. But if it's not possible, make sure you do not put yourself in a questionable position.

1. Don't act like a traffic cop; hand stretched out like you are stopping traffic.
2. Don't draw the wrong attention to yourself.

3. But if you are trying to gather a group of people in the open then you will want to draw positive attention to yourself. But, when ministering individually or in a small group we need to remember our attention is always on the one we are ministering to at the moment. Sometimes, Holy Spirit comes upon people in a strong way and might cause them to shake or begin to fall. That's okay. But for you ministering, if Holy Spirit begins to make you shake, fall over or make loud sounds then it would be good to withdraw from everyone if you can't control your body. (I'm not saying you can't flow with the Spirit but I am saying use wisdom and think about others around you).

4. Try to refrain from religious jargon which may alienate the people around you.

5. Christians routinely use words like "sin," "salvation," "fellowship," "sanctification," and "the gospel" without realizing these phrases can leave their friends confused or even repelled. So, choose your words carefully.

6. I also recommend that you don't take gifts or donations for healings. Kindly decline it in a way that will not offend them. You can thank them for their generosity and explain that the gifts God gives are free. When you give them a personal or ministry contact card and if your website has a donation button and they want to bless you, let them do it because the Spirit has put it in their hearts and they can do it on their own time and not during ministry.

7. Don't feel that you have to minister to everyone, this is a lifestyle and not an event. Be like Jesus, when you feel compelled then step out.

8. It's ok to pray for Holy Spirit to touch them and for the increase of His presence through you. Be on the lookout for any opportunity.

9. Don't shout when you pray!

10. Don't pray in tongues.

11. People will think you are crazy and run away from you. Now if the Holy Spirit leads you to pray for someone to receive tongues, just be aware of your surrounding and find a place that won't freak people out. Do it in a way that will not draw

attention to yourself and others. We want this to be a special moment not an embarrassing moment.

We do encourage prophetic ministry but don't be negative, keep it positive according to 1 Corinthians 14:3.

When Praying:

First note that praying for the spiritually lost in the marketplace or in the streets is different from praying for a believer in a building or church. If all you have done in the past is pray for believers, then you have to learn how to pray differently. Don't use religious jargon. Also, when in a mall, don't be too noticeable. If security approaches, remember you are shopping, looking around and enjoying the mall. This is a lifestyle not an evangelistic event. Don't say I'm praying for people, security will kick you out. Just shop and enjoy the day.

I encourage you to keep your eyes open and always be aware of your team members who might be hearing God or want to agree with you in prayer.

If you are seasoned in marketplace ministry, always be ready to break the ice for new people so that they can have a chance to step out.

Note: Men, I encourage you not to touch a woman. Ideally, men pray with men and women with women unless you are by yourself. Men should be very careful when laying hands to pray for women. Never lay your hands on a woman's breasts or stomach or hold her hand. You should not pat, stroke or rub while praying. Make sure your hands rest gently on the person. In most cases you don't even need to touch them. Again, always ask for permission.

I recommend that when praying for someone in a wheelchair, never drag them out of the chair and declare they are healed. If they give you a sign through words or actions that they feel better, then ask them if they would like to try walking. Assure them that you are there to help them and it will be ok. If they say no then let them know they don't have to. Remember in most cases if they were instantly healed,

God will also give them power to get up and walk. But if they want to try and walk there is nothing wrong with assisting them at first and ask how they feel and let them declare their own healing.

Prayer Guidelines:

1. Prayer of peace and knowledge of God's love.
2. Once you have made a prayer of command over a condition or situation, pray for God's peace to be released into the person and for them to experience God's love. You now have the opportunity to share whatever Holy Spirit is saying about this person. If you're in a group, keep eye contact with other team members as they may have something more to add.
3. Exercise faith.
4. Once you have finished praying, get the person to test their healing. (Remember the teaching we went through about how healing comes)?
5. If they are instantly healed tell them to thank God and share their story.
6. At this time, if they are with friends or family and someone else has pain, let the person who encountered healing lay hands and command the pain to go in Jesus name.
7. Note: I never encourage people to stop taking their medications if they feel they have been healed. Tell them to go to the doctor first for a checkup and let the doctor advise them on how to come off the medication. Also, it's a great way for people to share their testimony of how they got healed.

When Using A Camera:

The best moments to capture are when you are ministering healing. Let the person know you are filming for training purposes. If they decline and then are healed after you pray for them then ask if they would be willing for you to record their testimony so others can be encouraged by their healing.

Simple Approaches to Break the Ice:

1. When there is more than one person in your group you can say: "Hey I got a question for you, do you know what this person does? Point to one of your team members when you say this. The person will say something like "I don't know what they do?" Then say: "Well it's hard to explain but let me show you, do you have any pain in your body?

2. Maybe the person has an obvious injury. Ask: "Hey what happened? Let them talk. Then say, "That looks so painful. On a scale of 1 to 10, ten being the worst, what is your pain level?" After they respond tell them, "Let me show you something" and you or someone in your group can point to the pain and command it to go. After the command ask the person what their pain level is again.

3. You can also ask the person if they need a miracle in their life.

4. A magic trick can also be a good ice breaker. If you don't know any trick you can easily learn one from YouTube. Approach the person and ask if they like magic tricks, most people usually say yes. Show them your trick and when they ask, "How did you do that?" tell them you have something really cool and ask if they have any pain in their body.

5. A good joke is also a great ice breaker. Ask the person, "Have you heard this joke?" When you are through telling the joke, you can ask if they have any pain in their body or medical issues.

6. You can give a gift of a flower, pen or a poem. After breaking the ice, hand them the object whether a pen or flower. While they are holding the object ask them about any pain they have or health issues. After praying and ministering to them ask them to check their pain level. If you have written a poem, tell them you have it and you would like to hear their opinion and ask if you can share it with them. If they say yes read the poem and afterwards tell them "these are words of encouragement, just speaking life into you" then ask them to check the pain.

What Next After Breaking the Ice?

1. Start by asking where does it hurt on their body?
2. Matthew 20:32: Jesus stopped and called them and asked "What do you want me to do for you?" (NKJV). Ask about their level of pain and listen carefully to what they are saying. Also listen to the Holy Spirit and let Him guide you.
3. Explain that you want to lay hands on them while you pray.
4. Luke 4:40: When the sun was setting, the people brought to Jesus all who had various kinds of sickness, and laying His hands on each one, He healed them.
5. Mark 16: 17,18: and these signs will accompany those who believe. They will place their hands on the sick people and they will get well.
6. Note: Always ask for permission to lay your hands on someone before you pray. Don't place your hands on inappropriate places.
7. Release Holy Spirit in you to manifest.
8. Luke 5:17: and the power of the Lord was present for him to heal the sick. Keep your eyes open as you release from you the presence of Holy Spirit. Watch for signs of the Spirit manifesting; trembling, fluttering eyelids, shaking, heat, tears, sheen to the face, laughter, deep sense of peace. There are so many ways the Spirit can manifest.
9. The prayer of authority.

Examples from Jesus:

> *Mark 1:41: Filled with compassion, Jesus reached out his hand and touched the man. 'I am willing,' Jesus said 'be clean.'"*

> *Matthew 10:1: He called the 12 disciples to him and gave them authority to drive out evil spirits and to heal every disease and sickness.*

> *Matthew 17:20: He replied, 'Because you have so little faith. I tell you the truth, if you have faith as small as a mustard seed, you can say to this mountain move from here*

to there and it will move, nothing will be impossible for you.'

Acts 3:6: Then Peter said 'silver or gold I do not have, but what I have I give you. In the name of Jesus rise up and walk.

Take authority over the condition and speak a word of command. For example, "I command (name the condition) to go in the name of Jesus. I command cancer to go now, we reverse this cancer and the damage it has caused, be healed!"

APPENDIX B:

ONE-ON-ONE EVANGELISM

Mastering the Art of Kindness

Kindness unlocks doors we never knew existed and breaks barriers that lead to victory. In this section, I am going to show you how to activate this gem when ministering to people in the marketplace, workplace or anywhere the Lord leads you.

You can practice this by taking some time during your day to day life and step out. Begin with the mindset that you are going to find people to show God's love to through simply building friendship.

For example, let's say you are in a store buying something and you see a person next to you. Say hello or compliment them on something about themselves or what they are wearing. You can say "I like your hat or watch" etc. That's a good way to start a conversation but remember your agenda shouldn't center around only on healing/prophetic ministry unless the opportunity presents itself. You are simply out to learn how to approach people with the aim of starting a conversation. Keep in mind that you are not setting out to convert them or lay hands on them, but your goal is to show love and kindness through your conversation.

Remember to be yourself, don't try to be like Missionary PaulyB or a big-name evangelist. Just be you. You have nothing to prove. This isn't about performance or a formula – it's about love. So just let people see the real, imperfect, flawed, quirky, weird, beautiful and magical person that you are.

Always remember the people you come in contact with are living life and facing various challenges and difficulties just like you. Some could be discouraged or hurting. Statistics say 75 per cent of

Americans are not happy with their lives or how things are going. So, when you say or do something nice, it brings a moment of joy into their lives and it means a lot.

Some people may not know how to deal with kindness so they may react a little rude. It's only because they are not used to it or they could think you are trying to get something from them. However, know that their response is not about you so don't take their reaction personally. They are simply not used to people being nice or showing acts of love to them.

I want you to keep this in mind: The Gospel works in any situation. One day I was walking on the street and there was a lady walking towards me. I heard the Holy Spirit tell me to speak to her and tell her that she is amazing. That was it? It seemed rather lacking so I asked the Holy Spirit, "Is there anything else besides she is amazing?!" He told me, "No. Just tell her that." And so, as she approached I said, "Ma'am, I just want to let you know that God wants me to tell you that you are amazing." She looked me in the eyes and didn't say anything as tears started to build up in her eyes and roll down her cheeks. She asked me, "How did you know that?" I told her I was just hearing God's voice. He wanted me to tell you.

She began to tell me how 30 minutes earlier she had fought with her spouse who told her to leave and that she was ugly, stupid and could never have a better life. She said as she left her house she looked up to heaven and said "God why did you make me to be a failure and ugly? I hate my life, I'm so worthless I want to die." She cried together on the street corner because God had heard her cry, saw her pain and used me to tell her that she was amazing.

I was able to touch her life because I was willing to stretch my faith and tell her one nice thing about herself. This changed her whole outlook on life, herself and her view of God. She knew God was real that day all because of one simple word. I want you to notice the power behind the simplicity of this prophetic word. There was no difficult thing like knowing a social security number, birthday or address. It was simply saying, "You are amazing." The point I'm making is God knows where each person is at in life and He knows what details they need revealed to them.

Most of us know all that churchy stuff. Like how to act, how to perform, and how to make everything fall into a system and formula. I'm not saying church function is bad, but my point is that we must learn to just be ourselves because we are children in the kingdom. My heart's desire is to make this as easy as possible in order to motivate you to step out and be all that God created you to be in Him.

If you are too scared to speak to someone then begin by smiling and waving at them. Continue doing this when you are out and about and eventually you will build confidence. You can begin to incorporate a greeting as you wave and smile. After practicing that for a while, take it a step further and add a compliment to the greeting e.g. "Hello, wow, that's a nice car you have." For a lady you might say, "I love your purse, where did you get that? Just simple conversation. But remember this is about building relationships, friendship and nothing more than that.

Another thing you can do is to take a $20 bill and break it up into $5's. Then go to the streets and ask the Holy Spirit to lead you to someone in need. Look for homeless people who might be holding a sign asking for help. Walk up to them and say, "Hi. How are you? I noticed your sign asking for help. Can I ask what your story is and what's going on with you?" If you ever engage in a conversation and get lost in not knowing what to talk about, look for something they are wearing or have with them to talk about. Get them talking about themselves. A majority of people love to talk about themselves so it's an easy way to keep a conversation alive.

So, as you listen to the person's story, take note of key things they are saying and probe them further about it. In the art of love, asking and listening are a major tool when doing ministry. After engaging in small talk and breaking the ice, you could even offer buying them lunch and then give them $5. You can end it there or ask them if there is anything you can pray for them about.

After opening up a conversation most people likely will open up to you and agree to being ministered to. The biggest reason why a stranger may reject you is because they do not know you and might be wondering what the catch is or why you are being nice to them.

Another way to start a conversation is when you are checking out at a store. Compliments go a long way because most people don't get them often enough and they love to hear them. Or even when standing in line at the store you can smile and be nice to the people also waiting. Try to engage with as many people as possible.

These exercises will begin to help you overcome mental blocks you might have and it will slowly remove the barrier keeping you from engaging others. These blocks or walls are not only unique to ourselves. Many people erect them for protection which isolates them in a bubble. People need to break out of that protective bubble and your kindness is the needle that bursts it. Love always penetrates the heart.

Approach people confidently as if you know them. What's funny is that they will look at you and wonder how you know them. But by the time they figure out that you are a stranger then it's too late and they will have warmed up to you.

Remember that God is reconstructing any wrong mindsets we might have. Holy Spirit cleans up our perspective of how we see God. Sometimes we get so caught up in gaining ground in the marketplace that we forget Holy Spirit wants to reveal Himself through the process.

One of the fruits of the Spirit is self-control. Holy Spirit wants us to learn to master our mind and thoughts through self-control. Our mindset is what often keep us from stepping out and doing what God has called us to do. Whether if we feel we are an evangelist or not, we are all called to share our faith with others.

Here are some things I personally have to remind myself about on a daily basis. One is that Christ is in me, Jesus is my identity and that the hope of Glory is in me. (Colossians 1:27). Glory represents God's presence, power, authority and His atmosphere. So, you're revealing

His Glory and bringing hope through acts of love, kindness, healing and prophesy. The world is groaning and longing for a manifestation of the sons and daughters of God.

I know the toughest part is stepping out. But John 8:36 says he whom the Son sets free is free indeed. See, the first thing we need to be set free from isn't necessarily fear or rejection but to be free from self. I tell people that the all-time biggest enemy isn't the devil but it is self. We worry about what people will think about us or say about us. We ask what if I pray for someone and they don't get healed? What if I step out to prophesy and I miss it, or I'm telling people Jesus can heal but we don't see it manifest. The root of all these questions and fears is self. We don't want to be seen as people who are incompetent failures or appear as phony. The root to rejection is self.

Colossians 3:1-3 says that as sons and daughters of God, our minds need to be renewed into the mindset of Christ. Having Christ's heavenly mindset means keeping our minds on what is above and not on the earth. Verse 3 says we have died and our life is in Christ. And the next verse goes on to say that when Christ appears in you, you will appear with Him in His glory.

Colossians 1:27 talks about Christ in you the hope of glory. See, it's a process to learn to walk in this, to grow and learn to reckon ourselves dead and to be set free from false thinking of self and God.

Most of the time we get caught up in developing our giftings rather than dealing with our identity and letting God renew things in our lives. With that said, it's not so much about what God has called us to do, but who God has called us to be. Everyone has a different journey where learning to walk this out will take time while others will quickly catch on. This is because everyone has their own personality and obstacles to overcome. What will help us through this is to be sensitive to the voice of God.

You will come across people who are reserved and laid back, some who are nice, some might be super rude or obnoxious, some who are vocal, outspoken and loud. When you are sensitive to the Holy

Spirit, He will give you words from heaven that you can release into each type of person. God created everyone in their own uniqueness and Holy Spirit will lead you with each person.

Learning to rest in Jesus and His abilities and to flow from that place will take the pressure off of you. I find some people have a passive nature and there is nothing wrong with that. But, sometimes people who are outspoken and active can cause some people to feel overwhelmed. Or they might look at well-known speakers who minister with ease and it makes them step back thinking, "I can't do that or I can't be like that". God made you to be the best of you. Your approach will be different than everyone else's and that's ok, because not everyone is aggressive. But I do encourage you from time to time to push yourself beyond your comfort zone. This will break your own barriers and allow others to come into your circle. After all, isn't Holy Spirit the Comforter? So, when you are uncomfortable He will then comfort you.

Let me tell you, your greatest weapon in life isn't your gifts but the Spirit's fruit. (Galatians 5:22-23). Any of your daily activities can be amazing opportunities to exercise the Spirit's fruit God has placed inside you. So, allow it to flow.

Remember that you are not going out only to pray for the sick. This is not an event but a lifestyle. Approach people as opportunity presents itself. We aren't out on the prowl for people to pray for; it isn't stalker evangelism! It's about a lifestyle of making friends everywhere we go.

This isn't even about preaching to get people saved, though the opportunity for that will be there. Remember the greatest love understood is the love acted out.

It can be easy to get into the numbers game e.g. today I got five people saved or I prayed for ten people to be healed. We can't forget these are simple people with real needs and issues. They are not statistics where we forget their names and merely walk away with amazing testimonies. We can give them the love-encounter they long for with the Father.

Always give the people your name. You don't have to say I'm with a church or organization, let the people get to know you first. Don't be discouraged when people don't receive you. Don't take offence. They could be busy or late or they just don't know how to handle people who are boldly approaching them. Don't let the negative mindset creep in.

Tips on Overcoming Rejection and Approaching People Door to Door

In this book, I have touched on stuff you won't find in church or at your weekly Bible study.

This is why I am giving you the tools you need to be who God has called you to be as a lifestyle and not an event.

If you are a beginner, I encourage you to go with someone. Iron sharpens iron, so you will be able to encourage one another and it creates a fun experience. Also, being in a group at first helps you become bold faster and builds confidence to take the step to bring someone into the kingdom.

This is one of the most powerful mission fields out there. It has many successes and it is a great way to reach people, build a home group or church. I'm going to give you a couple of quick tips that if used you'll see some amazing results.

When approaching a house, the ideal scenario is to have a male and female. You can also do it on your own but it is recommended that you go door to door in pairs. Always have a contact card that you can leave wherever you go. You can tell the people that in case of an emergency and they need prayer you'll be there for them and they should feel free to contact you.

Ice Breakers to Use When Going Door to Door:

Knock on the door and introduce yourself by name and say you are in the neighborhood seeing how you can be of help to people. Introduce the person you are with and offer to help the people for free. What this does is to get your foot inside the door from where you can start building a relationship. But don't be too quick to ask to pray unless you don't want to use this method. This method will get you plugged into so many new relationships that later you can ask to pray or prophesy over their life.

Another approach is to knock on the door and after introductions tell them you were in the neighborhood blessing people. Ask if they need a miracle in their life or a situation and say, "we would like to agree in prayer with you."

You can also say you are giving away a free gift of healing. You can say "my partner here has an incredible gift, they have the ability to take people's pain away. It's a free gift, do you have any pain in your body?

You can say, "We are encouraging people in the neighborhood and would like to take a minute and give you an encouraging word."

APPENDIX C

FAITH DECLARATIONS

We are in the image and likeness of God, therefore:

- (Your name) in Jesus is a royal priesthood.

- (Your name) in Jesus is anointed.

- (Your name) in Jesus is alive to God.

- (Your name) in Jesus is the apple of God's eye.

- (Your name) in Jesus all grace abounds for you.

- (Your name) in Jesus, as He is, so are you on earth like God.

- (Your name) in Jesus is baptized into one Spirit.

- (Your name) in Jesus you are wise.

- (Your name) in Jesus you are worthy of the Father.

- (Your name) in Jesus you are wonderful.

- (Your name) in Jesus you are perfected.

- (Your name) in Jesus, you are His beloved.

- (Your name) in Jesus you are blessed with all spiritual blessings.

- (Your name) in Jesus you have bold access to the throne room.

- (Your name) in Jesus you are bold as a lion because you're born of God.

- (Your name) in Jesus you are purified.

- (Your name) in Jesus you're raised with Christ in God.

- (Your name) in Jesus you are the redeemed of God

- (Your name) in Jesus you are part of the Bride of Christ.

- (Your name) in Jesus you can do all things through Christ.

- (Your name) in Jesus you are chosen by God.

- (Your name) in Jesus all His fullness dwells in you.

- (Your name) in Jesus you are a co-heir with Christ.

- (Your name) in Jesus you are created for God's good work.

- (Your name) in Jesus you are curse free.

- (Your name) in Jesus you are demon free.

- (Your name) in Jesus you are dead to sin.

- (Your name) in Jesus you are holy.

- (Your name) in Jesus you are the righteous of God.

- (Your name) in Jesus you are a teacher.

- (Your name) in Jesus you are the elect of God

- (Your name) in Jesus you are enriched.

- (Your name) in Jesus everything works in your favor.

- (Your name) in Jesus you are enriched in all knowledge.

- You are free from sin.

- You are free in Christ.

- He has given you all things.

- You are fruitful.

- You are gifted.

- You are given all things.

- You are the habitation of God.

- You are lacking in nothing.

-You are a saint.

- You are a son of God.

- You are the salt of the earth.

- You are glorified.

- You are sanctified.

- You have the mind of Christ.

- He is at work in you.

- He is for you not against you.

- You are healed.

- You are hidden in Christ.

- You are highly favored.

- You are His body.

- You are His passion.

- You are His workmanship.

- You are a holy nation.

- You share in His authority.

- You are a servant.

- You are increasing in the knowledge of God.

- You are inseparable from the love of God.

- You are justified.

- The Kingdom of God is within you.

- You are a king and priest.

- You are a ruler.

- You are known by Him.

- You are the light of the world.

- You are living by faith.

- You live by God's word.

- You are a living stone.

- You are made in His image.

- You are rich in everything.

- You are more than a conqueror

- You have a sound mind.

- You are ordained.

- You are different.

- You are the people of God.

- You are prepared for God's work.

- You are protected.

- You are saved.

- You are sealed.

- You are seated with Him.

APPENDIX D

PROPHETIC SYMBOLS DICTIONARY

Prophetic Symbols Guide

Each person needs to learn the language that God uses to speak to them. I personally learned through pictures, images, colors and numbers. It was quite a journey to learn what these things mean. I have put together a short prophetic dictionary and I encourage you to do your own. But the one I'm sharing hopefully will help you in your journey in learning how to hear God through images, numbers and colors. However, take note that as much as it has worked for me, it might not be the case for you.

It has taken hours of my own personal study time to put together this Prophetic Symbol Dictionary. Many times, we get metaphors, pictures, visions or see things we can't make out. We must remember that there is always context behind the symbol. This is what helps you put the pieces of prophesy together in a whole. Some symbols can change from time to time. But the Holy Spirit will reveal to you.

Actor: Someone who is known, or a call to greatness, can represent a role they are playing.
Air plane crash: Moving from one season into another season.

Airplane: Someone who carries people, a leader, can mean an organization, job, ministry or business. The size of the plane makes a difference to the impact.
Animals: Characteristics, gifting, attacks that depend on the type of animal.
Ankles: Flexibility, movement, connection.

Ape or Monkey: Crazy, fun, good instincts.

Arm: Strength or connection.

Attic: The past, neglected, stored, hidden away.

Baby: Something new such as a job, gifting, idea.

Back: The past, vulnerability, family values.

Bank: Money, finances, provision.

Bankruptcy: Depleted, old season coming to an end, new start.

Basement: Hidden or beneath the surface, foundational issues or values.

Bat: Demonic attack, involves fear.

Bathroom: Cleansing, flushing, healing.

Bear: Demonic attack, unusual strength.

Beaver: Staying busy, steadiness.

Bed, Bedroom: Intimacy, closeness, rest.

Bee, Hornets, Wasp: Demonic attack, painful times, bee can represent gifting because they make honey.
Bicycle: Leisure, recreation, small impact ministry or job.

Birds: Depends on the type of bird.

Blackbird, Raven: Undercover, demonic attack or negative influence.

Blouse: Gifting, talents, covering.

Boat: Organization or personal job or ministry, depends on the boat.

Battleships: Spiritual warfare.

Books or Bookshelves: Information, revelation, education, writing.

Boots: Boldness, able to go places, walk through tough times.

Bride: Group of Christians, the Church, wife, love.

Bridge: Transition, season of change.

Buffalo: Fierce, provision, fake you out (as in to buffalo you).

Building: Depends on the type of building and context.

Bull: Stubbornness, mean, attack.

Bus: Small group of people, business, church, ministry, city-oriented or local.

Butterfly: Come through transformation, beauty, delicate.

Camel: Perseverance, able to get through tough and dry times, connection to the Middle-East

Car: Various aspects of your life, family, personal job, or ministry, remember to watch for context in order to understand details.

Cartoon character: Fun, consider character's name or function.

Cat: Independence, strong-willed, sly, creative. But a **Black cat:** Possible occult spirit.

Cave: Isolation, alone time, hidden.

Ceiling: Topped out, unable to grow higher, limited, rising higher.

Cemetery: Old things, dying to the past, family and generational calling.

Chair: Position, rest.

Chicken: Food, provision, afraid.

Cliff: Bigger vision, edge, risk.

Clock: Might be the numbers on the clock meaning something, timing, time.

Closet: Prayer time, hidden, storing away.

Coat: Call to action, mantle, talents, and gifts.

Coffin: Loss, dying to the old, new season ahead.

Coins or change: Foreign Coins: Influence or connection in those counties, money, change, favor.

Cow: provision, slow moving.

Credit Card: Finances, borrowed favor, given favor, debt.

Crossroads: change, decisions.

Cruise ship: Fun times, relaxation.

Cup: Calling, refreshing.

Dam: Things being held back, power.

Dart: Attack.

Death, Dying: Overcoming things, leaving one season and moving to another.

Debt: Overextended, trap or impaired, repayment.

Deceased relatives: Bringing wisdom and advice, healing from grief, fulfill the family calling.

Deer: Gentle spirit, thirsty for spiritual things, food.

Desert: Dry time, wilderness.

Desk: Calling, your job, writing, business.

Diamond: Under pressure to succeed, high value, beauty, influence.

Dinosaur: Old ways of thinking, dry religious spirit.

Doctor: Healing ministry, Jesus (healer), medical calling, need healing.

Dog: Friends, love, companionship.

Dolphin: Fun, able to refresh others.

Donkey: Carries the load, not too smart, stubborn.

Door: Opportunity, transition.

Dove: Holy Spirit, hope.

Dragon: Demonic attack, mystical.

Dragonfly: Spiritual warfare gift, something holding you back from flying.

Duck: Provision, letting things go, lay low.

Eagle: Insight, prophesy.

Earthquake: Turbulent times, radical change, warning of a coming disaster.

Egg: New understanding, growth, ideas, creation.

Elbow: Flexibility, push through, working hard.

Elephant: Old thoughts and memories, major influence, making a big impact.

Elevator, lift: New levels, advancement, decrease, easy season.

Eyes: Prophetic gifting, spiritual perception, seer, clarity.

Ear: Prophetic gifting, perception, listener.

Face: Your true self, identity, honor, self-image.

Family: Family values, past issues, generational callings to fulfill, negative connections that hold you back.

Fashion: Elegance, beauty, influence.

Feet: Foundation, daily life or walk, support.

Fence: Division or protection

Fingers: Direction, connection, gifting depending on the finger:

1. **Thumb:** Change, administrative.

2. **Index:** Prophetic, give direction.

3. **Middle:** Evangelistic, sales oriented, offensive.

4. **Ring finger:** Compassionate, pastoral.

5. **Pinky:** Teacher, instructor.

Fire: Enthusiasm, destruction, God's power and Spirit, passion.

Fish: Sport, people, gift to help others, outreach oriented.

Flies: Demonic attack, small and pesky.

Floods: Something on the move, major move of the Spirit, cleansing of the old ways, destruction.

Flowers: Growth, beauty, making beautiful, gift of encouragement.

Fog: Unclear times.

Food: Nourishment, spiritual growth, service, fun, community and relationship.

Forehead: Steadfast, mindset, belief systems.

Fox: Attack that can be undetected, rob your efforts, attractive women or men.

Frog: Attack against sexuality, lust, able to adapt.

Front: Vision, future.

Fruit: Spiritual food, gifts, characteristics, spiritual qualities.

Funeral: Ending one season, death, change coming.

Garage: Storage, rest from job or ministry, take a break, hold back.

Garden: Growth, provision, character.

Gas station: Refreshment, refuel, time of being filled and renewed.

Gate: New opportunity, spiritual connections.

Gifts: Talents, promotional times, surprises.

Giraffe: High minded, thinker, able to rise above, connect with God.

Glasses; Contact lens: Vision, insight, needs some type of help to see more clearly.

Goat: Negative person, not a true friend, untrustworthy, gullible.

Gold: Purity, refining process, holiness, finances.

Grapes: Gifts, refreshments, spiritual food.

Grass: Growth.

Gun: Authority, spiritual warfare, protection.

Hair: Wisdom, strength, beauty.

Hallway: Transition.

Hand: Relationship, reaching out.

Hat: Covering, protection.

Head: Mind and thinking, renewed, authority.

Heart: Compassion, love.

Heel: Vulnerability, resist.

Helicopter: Similar to plane: Aspect of life, job and ministry but much more mobile.

High-rise: Major life calling.

Hippo: Someone with a big mouth, hurts many people.

Hips: Identity, passion.

Honey: The goodness of God, nourishment, Spiritual gifts, God's presence.

Hospital: Healing, healing ministry, or profession.

Hot air balloon: Slow moving time, leisure, rise above things.

Hotel, Motel: Temporary time, transition.

House: Aspects of your life, family, job, ministry.

House: Various aspects of your life, family, job ministry:

1. **Living room:** Relational, fellowship, community, new life.

2. **Kitchen:** Place of preparation, nourishment, food.

3. **Bathroom:** Flushing, cleansing, healing.

4. **Dining room:** Spiritual growth and food.

5. **Basement:** Hidden, beneath the surface, foundational issues.

6. **Garage:** Rest from job or ministry, not using talents, store up.

7. **Attic:** The past, neglected, stored.

8. **Den:** Family room, community or fellowship, family oriented.

9. **Bedroom:** Intimacy, restoration.

10. Porch: Community, recreation, leisure.

11. Backyard: Past, play time.

12. Closet: Stored away, hidden, time of personal prayer.

Hummingbird: Gentleness, delicate.

Ice: A move of the Spirit that will come later, slippery times.

Incense: prayer and intercession, healing, the goodness of God.

Insects: Demonic attack, more of a nuisance, pesky.

Jewels: Gifting, life calling or purpose, family and generational inheritance, spiritual gifts.

Judge: God, mediator, justice.

Kangaroo: Unstable or bouncy times, ups and downs, comfort.

Ketchup: "Catch up," running behind.

Key: Opportunities, strategies, authority.

Kiss: Tenderness, passion, love, similar, gifting as the person you kiss, lust.

Knee: Prayer, flexibility, humility.

Knife: Spiritual warfare, authority, attack.

Ladder: Advancement, promotion, opportunities.

Lamb: Sacrifice, young Christian.

Lamp: Guidance, insight, angelic.

Lawyer: Justice, defender, mediator, advocate.

Legs: Your "walk" or daily life, advancement, strength.

Lettuce: Play on words: "Let us," (ask for more), nourishment, spiritual food.

Library: Learning, wisdom, knowledge.

Lighthouse: Spiritual guidance, keeps you from danger.

Limousine: Elegance, influence.

Lion: Power, strength, God, lion of the tribe of Judah, can also represent the enemy.

Lips: Tenderness, speech, articulate talker.

Lock: Opportunity for later, blocked, guarded.

Locust: Spiritual attack normally on finances, demonic attack.

Mansion: Influence, riches, kingdom of God, heaven.

Map: Strategy, plan, guidance.

Marketplace: Business, interacting, with others, financial gain.

Marriage: Covenant or promise, commitment, family, partnership.

Meat: Nourishment, spiritual food, maturity.

Mechanic: Repairing things in your life, career,

Military Planes: Served in the air force or a calling to the military or even spiritual warfare.
Mirror: Self-image, self-esteem, vision.

Money: Finances, provision, wealth, favor.

Monster: Demonic attack, usually with fear.

Moon: Guidance during dark times, reflections, God's lighthouse

Motorcycle: Similar to Car: Some aspect of your life, your job, ministry, but more mobile

Mountain: Higher calling or destiny, intimate time with God.

Naked: Open, transparent, vulnerable, freedom.

Night: Unclear times.

Oasis: Refreshing after a dry time, rest.

Ocean: Large move of the Spirit, humanity, great leader, influence, many people.

Office building: Business, job, life calling.

Oil: Holy Spirit, the spiritual realm, healing, anointing.

Old Man: Old behaviors, things you once overcame, the old nature, an old person.

Owl: Wisdom and discernment.

Panther: Power (negative or positive), independence.

Path: Life's journey, direction, road less traveled.

Peacock: Vibrant, pride.

Pearl: Something small that has great value, spiritual gifts formed beneath the surface.

Pictures: Visions, memories.

Pilot: Leader, Holy Spirit, guidance.

Plough: Preparing for something new, groundbreaker.

Police: Authority, good or bad. Protection, career.

Pregnant: Something new is coming like a job or gift, new ideas.

Rain: Blessing, refreshing time in the spirit, unclear time, move of God.

Rainbow: Covenant or promise of something new.

Reptiles: Possibly someone who is cold or mean.

Rocket: Advancement to higher things in the Spirit, moving fast.

Roses: Beauty, love, commitment.

School: Learning, education, spiritual training or if you go to school could be your life.

Rowboat: Slow moving with lots of effort.

Sailboat: Spirit-driven.

Seed: Growth, God's word, faith.

Shoes: Daily life and walk, peace.

Smoke: Presence of fire (could be positive) early sign of move of God, sign of danger, unclear times.

Snake: Lies and deception.

Snow: Move with the Spirit, recreation, revelation.

Songbird: Music, worship, joy and peace.

Speedboat: Acceleration, fun.

Stairs: Advancement, increase or decrease.

Submarine: Going deep in the things of the Spirit.

Suit: Business, leadership, person of influence.

Sword: Spiritual insight, defense.

Taxi: Temporary time, temporary worker.

Teeth: Wisdom, understanding, strength.

Telephone: Communication, prophetic.

Theatre: Creativity, big influence.

Tiger: Power and strength, (positive or negative), stubborn spirit.

Train: move of God, something new

Treasure: Riches, finances, hidden things, favor.

Tsunami: Large move of the Spirit, major impact, possible disaster.

Umbrella: Shields from attacks, protective covering.

Upstairs: Higher level, increase.

Valley: Difficult times.

Wallet/Purse: Identity, favor, finances.

Water: The Sprit, spiritual life, Holy Spirit, the spiritual realm, refreshment.

Wedding: Covenant, commitment, calling in life, marriage.

Window: Vision.

Wings: Able to rise above or get out of bad situations, angelic, high levels of creativity.

Colors: Can have positive and negative meanings.
1. **White:** Holiness, purity, religious.
2. **Silver:** Redemption, false humility.
3. **Blue:** Revelation, depression.
4. **Red:** Redemption, anger.
5. **Yellow:** Courage, caution, fear.
6. **Purple:** Authority, royalty, false authority.
7. **Black:** Neutral, hidden, dark or evil.
8. **Green:** Growth, misfortune.
9. **Brown:** Compassion, pastoral, humanism.

Numbers:
1. Single
2. Double
3. Trinity, God
4. Creativity, worldwide impact.
5. Grace
6. Man's efforts
7. Completion, perfection
8. New beginnings
9. Fruit of the Spirit and gifts; Judgment
10. Rules, law
11. Transition

12. Leadership, Covenant, 24 is the same

13. Rebellion

14. Establishment

15. 16 - High levels of grace

16. 18 - Provision, judgment.

17. 50 - Jubilee, reconciliation, freedom